Soup of the Day

365 Delicious Soup Recipes
for Every Day & Season of the Year

Soup of the Day

365 Delicious Soup Recipes
for Every Day & Season of the Year

Brad McCrorie

Fitzhenry & Whiteside

Fitzhenry & Whiteside Limited
195 Allstate Parkway
Markham, Ontario   L3R 4T8

In the United States:
121 Harvard Avenue, Suite 2
Allston, Massachusetts 02134

www.fitzhenry.ca   godwit@fitzhenry.ca

Fitzhenry & Whiteside acknowledges with thanks the Canada Council for
the Arts, the Government of Canada through its Book Publishing Industry
Development Program, and the Ontario Arts Council for their support of
our publishing program.

National Library of Canada Cataloguing in Publication

McCrorie, Brad
Soup of the day : 365 delicious, easy-to-follow soup recipes for every day
and season of the year / Brad McCrorie.

ISBN 1-55041-743-6

1. Soups.   I. Title.

TX757.M21 2003   641.8'13   C2003-903429-1

U.S. Publisher Cataloging-in-Publication Data
(Library of Congress Standards)
McCrorie, Brad.
Soup of the day : 365 delicious, easy-to-follow soup recipes
for every day and season of the year / Brad McCrorie.—1st ed.
[192] p. : cm.
Summary: 365 original soup recipes for master chefs or amateurs;
includes instructions on preparing stocks from scratch, and tips on
storing and freezing soups.
ISBN 1-55041-743-6 (pbk.)
1. Soups.   I. Title.
641.8/13 21   TX757.M33 2003

Cover Photograph: Corbis, First Light
Cover and interior design and typesetting by Kinetics Design
Printed and bound in Canada

Soup of the Day
Table of Contents

Soup of the Day

365 Delicious Soup Recipes
for Every Day & Season of the Year

 **Hot Soup – H**    **Cold Soup – C**   **Meal-in-a-Bowl – MIB**

Tried It	LOVED IT!		Kind	Serves	Page
		Asparagus Parmesan	H	12	108
		Mussel Pesto	H	8	108
		Lobster Basmati	H	8	109
		Chipolata Sausage	H	8	109
		Sirloin and Oysters	H	10	110
		Pike Bisque	H	10–12	110
		Quail with Cherries	H	10	111
		Tomato Tomato	H	8	111
		Lobster Mornay	H	10	112
		Italian Rib	MIB	12	112
		Spanish Crab	H	10	113
		Oxtail and Beans	H	6	113
		Cream of Onion and Garlic	H	10–12	114
		Smoked Turkey with Cheshire	H	8	114
		Stracciatella	H	10–12	115
		Cream of Zucchini and Eggplant	H	8–10	116
		French Vegetable and Cheshire Cheese	H	10–12	116
		Oyster Stew	H	8–10	117
		Chilled Peanut Butter with Frangelica	C	4–6	118
		Cantonese Braised Beef and Oyster	H	8–10	118
		Beef with Green Peppers	H	10–12	119
		Sicilian Meatball	H	8	120
		Italian Sausage	MIB	8–10	120
		Cajun Clams	H	6–8	121
		Mussel Stew – Café de Paris	H	10–12	122
		Mandarin Orange with Lime and Fresh Dill	C	6	122
		Cream of Fresh Basil	H	2–4	123
		Pineapple and Kiwi with Sherry	C	4–6	123
		Cream of Braised Lettuce	H	10–12	124
		Leek and Endive in Clear Broth	H	10–12	124
		Cream of Onion and Stilton Cheese	H	6–8	125
		Chicken Basmati	H	6–8	126
		Cooked, Chilled Gazpacho	C	8–10	126
		Scampi Stephanie	H	2–3	127
		Chervil	H	8	127
		Chicken Noodle	H	12–14	128
		Crabmeat Rarebit with Beer	H	14–16	128
		Scallop Mornay	H	8–10	129

Tried It	LOVED IT!		Kind	Serves	Page
		Drunken Squash	H	10	147
		Wild Boar Stew	MIB	12	147
		Beef Borscht	H	8	148
		Steak and Kidney with Red Wine	MIB	10	148
		Sugar Plum	C	4	149
		Good ol' Boys' Hog Chowder	H	8	149
		Chilled Sour Cherry	C	10	150
		Cajun Seafood	MIB	8–10	150
		Orange	C	4	150
		Zucchini Flowers with Cheese and Sun-Dried Tomatoes	H	6–8	151
		Bison Tenderloin	H	6–8	151
		Sour Cherries with Pork	H	8	152
		Curried Apple	C	10	152
		Smoked Duck with Swiss Chard	H	10	152
		Old Fashioned Short Ribs	MIB	8–10	153
		Veal with Mustard	H	10	153
		Buttermilk and Brie with Capers	H	6	154
		Tomato and Onion	H	8	154
		Honeydew	C	4–6	154
		Cheese and Eggs in Broth	H	8	155
		Spicy Chilled Scampi	C	6	155
		Mexican Bean	H	6–8	155
		Oysters in Bourbon and Cheese	H	4	156
		Crab and Tomato	H	6–8	156
		Mexican Tomato	H	6–8	156
		Cauliflower with Stilton	H	6	157
		Smoked Chicken Florentine	H	8	157
		Sour Mushroom	H	6–8	158
		Watermelon with Lime and Kiwi	C	4–6	158
		Enoki Mushroom and Pea	H	6–8	158
		Tomato with Couscous	H	6–8	159
		Greek Eggplant	H	8	159
		Ground Pork Szechuan	H	4–6	160
		Potato Dijon	H	6–8	160
		Chow Mein Soup with Pork	H	8–10	160
		Morels in Broth	H	6–8	161
		Lentils with Smoked Pork and Strawberries	H	6–8	161
		Scallops with Two Mushrooms in Red Wine	H	4	162

Introduction

"Your imagination and your taste buds may be the most important tools or gadgets in your kitchen."

Whenever I am asked – and just as often when I'm not, my friends will tell you – I am more than willing to expound loudly and at great length about what I consider to be the most delicious, nutritious, easy-to-prepare and satisfying meal ever invented.

That's soup, of course, and after more than 27 years in various kitchens, my passion for it continues to grow.

What other meal on the face of the planet gives you the freedom to mix and match ingredients with such wild abandon and inventiveness?

What other meal offers quite the same opportunity to test and taste your way through the cooking process, one sip, one tiny spoonful at a time, until the meal you are preparing tastes exactly the way you want it to taste?

What other meal gives you the opportunity to turn the very idea of *leftovers* into a brand new, magical treat for you and your family?

And finally, on those crazy days when the world is mad and there's too much to do, what other meal is the perfect solution when pizza, Chinese take-out, burgers or frozen foods begin to seem like the only answer?

1

The answer to all four questions, of course, is what this book is all about.

Did I mention economical?

In compiling the 365 recipes that give this book its title, I have naturally included more than a pot full of my own favorites, as well as the favorites of a number of my friends.

Rest assured, however, that there are recipes aplenty for everyone and every taste, and whether it's hot soup, cold soup, clear soup, cream soup, meat, poultry, game, vegetable soup or seafood chowder that you are looking for, read on.

(There's even a spot in the Table of Contents to mark the names and page numbers of favorites you discover in the pages of this book.)

I have also included a healthy selection of those dishes commonly referred to as meal-in-a-bowl – rich stews, ragouts, gumbos, and goulash.

Though the book is not divided by the seasons of the year, I have attempted to satisfy those appetites sparked by the seasons with recipes created to take advantage of the availability and abundance that our seasons bring.

If fresh salmon, lamb or fiddleheads put a spring in your step, you'll find them well represented throughout the book.

If, on the other hand, you'd walk a mile for the summertime thrill of chilled gazpacho, ice-cold cucumber, or vichyssoise – or climb over snow banks for a hearty soup of the meal-in-a-bowl variety – they're in here too.

"*Discover, Experiment, and Enjoy!*"

Variety being the spice of life, I have also chosen not to group the recipes by main ingredient, choosing instead to mix them randomly in an effort to encourage the reader to browse, discover, experiment and enjoy along the way. (Imagine a restaurant menu listing *soups of the day* – all made from beef!)

Being a fervent believer in experimentation, I urge my readers to do just that.

Approach each recipe the way a painter approaches a blank canvas, or the way a musician approaches a musical score. Think of the recipe as your basic guide; the art classes you took last summer, the sheet music to a favorite tune.

You have a picture in your mind's eye, or a tune in your head; now make it yours.

Remember, your imagination and your taste buds may be the most important tools or gadgets in your kitchen.

If two tablespoons of anything tastes better than one, then make it two.

If a half-cup of rum comes closer to the taste you are attempting to create (than say a quarter-cup) then so be it.

No recipe in this (or any other cookbook) is carved in stone.

As with my previous books, the recipes in *SOUP OF THE DAY* are inspired by cooking traditions far too numerous to list. Suffice it to say that when we sit down to eat, North Americans owe an enormous debt of gratitude to chefs from around the world, to people everywhere who have always and continue to interpret and re-interpret each other's cuisine.

And since nothing is more essential to good soup as homemade broth, I have included simple recipes for basic broths as well as tips for freezing and storing them.

As you browse the recipes in the following pages, keep an eye out for the graphic icons that quickly identify each soup by type:

 **Hot Soup – H**    **Cold Soup – C**

 **Meal-in-a-Bowl – MIB**

The final word, as it usually does, belongs to my mother, Gert McCrorie.

At home, or in restaurants where she has ruled the roost over the years, she has never placed a bowl of soup or any other kind of meal in front of a family member, or a lunchtime patron without wishing that person a cheery "Enjoy!"

Over the years, I've learned to do what she says.

I hope you will too.

Brad McCrorie
Toronto

Some Terms and Techniques

Adding Cheese or Eggs to Soup

Cheese is only added to cream soups or soups that contain plenty of ingredients for the cheese to cling to. Cheese is always grated before it is added to the boiling broth. Eggs must be added slowly with a whisk while the soup or stock is boiling. Soups may also be thickened without flour by a liaison of equal parts egg yolk and whipping cream (35%). This mixture should be added once the soup has been brought to a boil and whisked in slowly (not whipped) with the heat reduced to simmer.

Bouquet Garni

Make a small bag of cheesecloth, and fill it with thyme, basil, bay leaves, oregano and whole black peppercorns. The bouquet garni is a tidy and quick way of adding splendid seasoning to both soups and stocks.

Clarified Butter

This is butter from which the butter fat and milk solids have been removed. It is made by melting butter over a medium-high heat, then skimming off or straining the solids from the resulting liquid. Used for flavor and color when browning or frying, clarified butter gives the cook the ability to cook longer, at higher temperatures, without burning.

Commercial Bases

Time is an important ingredient in any cook's plans for dinner. Since few people have enough of it to devote to the proper reduction of the stocks used in the soup recipes in this book, there is no harm in adding one or two tablespoons of commercial base for added flavor when and where time and taste dictate.

Deglaze

Deglazing is a technique for removing all the drippings from a roasting pan. After the food has been removed from the roasting pan, pour wine or stock onto the pan while it is still hot. Scrape the mixture of wine or stock and remaining ingredients from the bottom of the pan and preserve this wonderful mixture. It can be added to a stock, or used as the essence of a sauce.

Dried Mushrooms

Some of the recipes featured in this book call for dried mushrooms. I use them simply because dried mushrooms are available all year round. Dried mushrooms should always be soaked for at least an hour at room temperature in water that has been brought to a rapid boil, then removed from the heat. Since the stems of dried mushrooms are apt to be tough, always trim the ends of the stems, or remove the stems altogether.

Freezing Soups

Since cream added to the stock in the preparation of creamed soups is apt to separate when frozen, it is best not to freeze creamed soups. However, you can always freeze the stock from which you plan to make a creamed soup. When the stock is thawed, add the cream to the stock as it comes to a boil. Since crisp vegetables will not be crisp when frozen and later reheated, and since eggs will discolor, clear soups should only be frozen after straining out these ingredients. Fresh vegetables or eggs can then be added, according to the recipe, once your stock has been thawed and brought to the proper temperature.

Reduction

Stocks, soups and even wines are reduced by simmering to increase, or concentrate their flavor. Reductions called for in each recipe (one-half reduction/one-quarter reduction) are achieved by simmering the liquid, uncovered, over a medium-high heat to the desired strength.

Roux

Light or dark, roux are easy to make and are often used to thicken soup. Both call for equal parts of butter and flour blended gently over a slow heat until the flour is cooked enough to rid it of its starchy taste. For the rich, nutty flavor of dark roux – used in thick, dark, and gamey soups – cook the roux over a medium-high heat until it turns a rich brown color.

Sauté, Sweat

To sauté is to cook food rapidly in hot butter or fat, turning and tossing it until it is golden brown, thereby sealing in the juices. To sweat is to bleed the juices from vegetables by stirring them gently in hot butter until they become translucent.

Serving Sizes

All the soups in this book will yield 9- to 10- ounce servings – perfect for lunch, pre-dinner, or a meal at any time.

Tomato Concassée

Only the meat of the tomato is used in concassée. To remove the seeds and skin, cut out the core of the tomato and make two shallow cuts just piercing the skin. Drop tomatoes into boiling water, and cook for one minute. Remove from the water and peel the skin away with a paring knife. The tomatoes will be quite hot, so wear rubber gloves. Cut the tomatoes in half and squeeze seeds out very gently. Dice the tomato meat, and the concassée is ready.

Unsalted Butter

Since the addition of salt to any food or soup is ultimately a matter of taste or diet, the recipes in this book were tested using unsalted butter. Salted butter, for those who prefer it, can be substituted.

Sauces, Stocks and Thickeners

Beurre Manié

Beurre manié is made with equal parts of whole butter and hard white flour, kneaded together until all the lumps disappear and it forms a smooth paste. It is a good idea for the serious cook to keep a pound of this excellent thickener in the refrigerator. When beurre manié is stored this way, it should be brought to room temperature before using. Since the flour is raw and apt to lump when added to hot liquids, one cup of the soup or stock should be added to the beurre manié a little at a time, stirring constantly until the mixture is consistent. It is then ready to be added to the cooking pot. Remember that raw flour needs to be cooked thoroughly to remove the starchy taste.

Demi-Glace or Basic Brown Sauce

Bring 2 L (8 cups) of a hearty beef stock to a boil. When stock reaches the boil, put a heavy frying pan on high heat. Heat 115 g (4 oz) of clarified butter in the frying pan, then add 115 g (4 oz) of hard white flour. Cook this roux until golden brown, and stir it constantly to avoid burning.

When brown, slowly ladle one cup of the stock into the hot roux, stirring constantly with a whisk to avoid lumps. When the stock and roux mixture has blended into a smooth paste, it can then be added to the stock. When the stock combination has returned to the boil, your demi-glace is complete.

Sauce Velouté

Bring either veal, chicken or fish stock to a boil. Slowly whisk in about 120 ml (1/2 cup) beurre manié to the boiling stock, until it reaches the thickness you desire. Remove from heat.

Stocks

Following are some basic recipes commonly called for in this book: beef stock, chicken stock and special fish, vegetable, poultry or game stocks.

Basic Beef Stock

Yields 3 Liters (12 cups)

1 1/2 kg (3 lbs)	beef bones
2	onions with skin, quartered
2	carrots, cut in **5 cm (2 inch)** pieces
3	garlic cloves
2	celery stalks, cut in **5 cm (2 inch)** pieces
30 ml (2 tbsp)	tomato paste
3 L (12 cups)	cold water

Preheat oven to 230° C (450° F).

Place bones in a shallow roasting pan. Roast in preheated oven until they begin to brown, about 30 minutes. Add onions, carrots, garlic, celery and tomato paste and continue to roast about 30 minutes more or until bones and vegetables are dark brown.

Combine browned bones and vegetables with water in a large stock pot. Bring to a boil over medium-high heat. Reduce heat to medium-low and simmer for 1 to 2 hours, skimming off the foam as it appears, and adding more water as necessary to keep the level constant. Strain out the bones and vegetables.

Note: For an even richer stock, oxtails can be used.

Basic Chicken Stock

Yields 3 Liters (12 cups)

2 kg (4 1/2 lbs)	chicken bones
2	onions with skin, quartered
3	carrots, cut in 5 cm (2 inch) pieces
3	garlic cloves with their skin
2	celery stalks, cut in 5 cm (2 inch) chunks
2	bay leaves
1 ml (1/4 tsp)	dried basil
1 ml (1/4 tsp)	dried oregano
1 ml (1/4 tsp)	dried thyme
7 1/2 ml (1 1/2 tsp)	white peppercorns
5	springs of parsley with their stems
4 L (16 cups)	cold water

Put chicken bones, onions, carrots, garlic, celery, bay leaves, basil, oregano, thyme, peppercorns and parsley into a large, heavy stock pot and cover with water. Bring to a boil over high heat, then immediately reduce heat to medium-low and simmer for 1 or 2 hours (or longer), skimming off the foam as it appears and adding water as necessary to keep the level constant. Strain out bones and vegetables and discard them.

Return stock to pot, raise heat to medium, and cook until stock has reduced by about a quarter, about 30 minutes.

Fonds Blanc, Veal or Chicken Stock

Quantities for all stocks are approximate. A pot that easily holds 4 L (16 cups) of water should yield about 3 L (12 cups) of stock. For veal stock, use shank bones. For chicken stock, use combinations of necks, backs, wings, legs and feet. For white stocks, do not brown the bones first.

Wash, peel and chop vegetables (onions, carrots, celery, garlic and leeks). Add a bouquet garni. Place all the ingredients in a large pot and cover with cold water. Place on top of the stove at high heat and bring to a boil. Reduce the heat and simmer for 2 hours or longer if you wish.

Strain stock and let it cool. Stock is now ready to be6 stored in portions in the refrigerator or the freezer for future use.

Fish Stock

Yields 3 Liters (12 cups)

1 kg (2 1/4 lbs)	grouper head
1–1 1/2 kg (2–3 lbs)	white fish or their bones
3	carrots, peeled and coarsely chopped
1	large spanish onion, peeled and coarsely chopped
6	large garlic cloves, peeled
10	white peppercorns
8	bay leaves
	salt to taste

Place all the ingredients into a large pot on top of the stove on high heat. Add cold water to cover ingredients by 2 1/2 cm (1 inch). Bring to a rolling boil. Remove from the stove and let stand for 20 minutes. Strain through a china cap, a fine-meshed, cone-shaped strainer, or use a colander.

Fond de Gibier or Game Stock for Game or Wild Fowl

Place about 1 kg (2 1/4 lbs) of game bones – preferably with marrow – on a flat baking tray and put into a preheated 230° C (450° F) oven for 1 hour to brown. Add a mirepoix, a mixture of sautéed vegetables made up of carrots, onion, celery and garlic that have been coarsely chopped, and bake for an additional 30 minutes. Remove, and reserve all the ingredients. Deglaze tray with red wine, and put this mixture into a pot that easily holds 4 L (16 cups). To the pot, add the bones and vegetables, along with 6 bay leaves, 20 juniper berries, 5 ml (1 tsp) thyme and 10 ml (2 tsp) tarragon. Fill the pot to several inches below rim with cold water and bring to the boil on high heat. When boiling begins, turn heat down and let simmer until reduced by one-third.

Cream of Watercress

Serves 4

1 bunch watercress
 – approx. **115 g (1/4 lb)**
1 vegetable stock cube
15 ml (1 tbsp) heaping, flour
240 ml (1 c) 35% cream

Trim discolored leaves from the watercress and discard. Roughly chop the watercress in a blender.

Add **480 ml (2 c)** cold water, the stock cube, and the flour.

Blend briefly until watercress is very finely chopped and ingredients are well mixed.

Pour resulting mixtures into a large pan and add **160 ml (2/3 c)** cream.

Bring to the boil over medium heat, stirring constantly.

Simmer for approximately 2 minutes.

Drip the remaining cream from the tip of a teaspoon to form a circle on each serving.

Draw the tip of a knife through each circle to form a heart shape.

Liz West's Shrimp Soup with Three Cheeses

Serves 6 – 8

115 g (1/4 lb) butter
35 – 40 peeled, de-veined shrimp
60 ml (1/4 c) peeled, chopped
 shallots
360 ml (1 1/2 c) fresh oyster
 mushrooms sliced
5 ml (1 tsp) chopped garlic
120 ml (1/2 c) Armangnac
240 ml (1 c) shrimp or fish stock
2 strands of saffron
1 1/2 L (6 c) fish or chicken velouté
60 ml (1/4 c) shredded Gorgonzola
 cheese
60 ml (1/4 c) Stilton cheese, shredded
60 ml (1/4 c) St. Agur cheese, grated

Put butter in your soup pot on high heat.

When butter is melted add shrimp, shallots and mushrooms and sauté on high for 5 minutes.

Add the garlic and cook while stirring until the garlic goes yellowish brown.

Then add the Armangnac and flambé – add the stock and reduce by half.

Add saffron and velouté and bring back to the boil.

Then whisk in cheeses until completely melted.

13

Spicy Lime Chicken
Serves 6

1 1/4 L (5 c) chicken stock
60 ml (1/4 c) chopped shallots
1 tomato, cored and chopped
1/2 yellow bell pepper, seeded and
    chopped
2 stalks lemongrass [available in
    Asian markets]
15 ml (1 tbsp) minced fresh ginger
1 fresh Serrano chili, stemmed and
    seeded
Kaffir lime leaves shredded
    [available in Asian markets]
2 whole boneless, skinless chicken
    breasts, halved
15 ml (1 tbsp) fresh lime juice
30 ml (2 tbsp) chopped fresh cilantro

Fried tortilla crisps and seasoned chili sauce make an excellent garnish.

Put the chicken stock, shallots, tomato, bell pepper, lemongrass, ginger, chili and lime leaves into a heavy soup pot over high heat, and bring to the boil.

Reduce heat and simmer for 20 minutes.

Add chicken breasts and continue to cook for 15 minutes or until chicken is cooked through.

Remove chicken breasts – shred meat and set aside.

Strain stock through a fine sieve, season with lime juice, return

to heat if necessary to warm to serving temperature.

Put equal portions of shredded chicken into each of 6 bowls, pour in stock.

Garnish with cilantro, fried tortilla crisps and chili sauce.

Classic Duck
Serves 6 – 8

30 ml (2 tbsp) olive oil
1 duck, skinned, boned and cut into
    8 pieces
60 ml (1/4 c) flour
480 ml (2 c) diced onions
240 ml (1 c) leek, white part diced
2 carrots diced
2 celery stalks diced
2 parsnips peeled and diced
2 L (8 c) duck or chicken stock
5 ml (1 tsp) chopped fresh tarragon
60 ml (1/4 c) brandy
360 ml (2 c) dry white wine
10 ml (2 tsp) green peppercorns in
    brine
15 ml (1 tbsp) Dijon mustard
30 ml (2 tbsp) red currant jelly
60 ml (1/4 c) "whitewash"
    (equal parts cornstarch and water)

Heat oil over medium heat in a large sauté pan.

Dredge duck in flour and brown well on all sides.

Set duck aside.

Add vegetables to pan and sauté for 5 to 6 minutes or until onions are translucent.

Add stock, tarragon, brandy, wine, peppercorns, mustard and red currant jelly, mix well and bring to the boil.

Return duck to pan, cover and simmer over low heat for 1–1/2 hours.

Combine cornstarch with **120 ml (1/2 c)** water and stir into soup.

Goulash
Serves 6 – 8

30 ml (2 tbsp) lard
460 g (1 lb) lean boneless stewing
    beef cut into **2 1/2 cm (1 in)** cubes
360 ml (1 1/2 c) onions chopped
1 clove garlic chopped
30 ml (2 tbsp) Hungarian sweet
    paprika
Dash of cayenne pepper
720 ml (3 c) beef stock
480 ml (2 c) water
5 ml (1 tsp) caraway seeds
5 ml (1 tsp) crumbled dried marjoram
480 ml (2 c) tomato concassée
240 ml (1 c) diced potatoes
240 ml (1 c) carrots sliced
2 sweet red peppers cut into chunks
45 ml (3 tbsp) "whitewash," in this
    case equal parts flour and water
Sour cream

Melt lard in your soup pot on high heat and add beef, browning well on all sides.

Remove from the pot with slotted spoon and reserve.

Add onions and garlic to the pot and cook 4 minutes, stirring occasionally.

Add paprika, cayenne, stock, **480 ml (2 c)** water, caraway, marjoram and reserved meat and bring to the boil while stirring well.

Reduce heat to low and cook covered for 45 minutes.

Add tomato concassée, potatoes, carrots, and red pepper.

Stir well and return to the boil, cover and cook for 30 minutes.

Add "whitewash" slowly to the soup, stirring well.

Cook over low heat, stirring until thickened.

Serve topped with sour cream.

French Provincial Oxtail

Serves 6 – 8

80 ml (1/3 c) clarified butter
1 1/2 kg (3 lbs) oxtails
120 ml (1/2 c) diced parsnip
120 ml (1/2 c) diced turnip
240 ml (1 c) diced onion
480 ml (2 c) diced green pepper
240 ml (1 c) diced carrot
240 ml (1 c) diced whole leek
15 ml (1 tbsp) chopped fresh
    tarragon
5 ml (1 tsp) fennel seeds
2 cloves garlic, minced
30 ml (2 tbsp) curry powder
20 sweet black olives pitted
120 ml (1/2 c) raisins
45 ml (3 tbsp) tomato paste
80 ml (1/3 c) mango chutney
240 ml (1 c) dry red wine
1 1/2 L (6 c) beef stock

Heat half the butter in a deep roasting pan over medium-high heat.

Add oxtails and brown well on all sides.

Remove meat from pan and set aside to cool.

Add remaining butter and heat until butter is smoking, add vegetables, tarragon, fennel seeds and garlic and sauté for about 3 to 4 minutes or until onions are limp.

Add curry, olives, raisins, tomato paste and chutney and mix well.

Add wine and stock and mix well.

Pick oxtail meat from bone, adding meat to your soup pot.

Cook on medium heat for approximately 3 hours or until meat is very tender.

Black Bean

Serves 8 – 10

480 ml (2 c) dried black beans
115 g (1/4 lb) lean salt pork
2 medium onions – one diced,
    the other whole
3 whole cloves
1 ml (1/4 tsp) mace
1/2 ml (1/8 tsp) cayenne pepper
120 ml (1/2 c) diced carrot
4 L (16 c) water
230 g (1/2 lb) thinly sliced lean beef
120 ml (1/2 c) sherry
3 hard boiled eggs, sliced
1/2 lemon, thinly sliced

Rinse beans and cover with water in your soup pot, soaking for one hour before draining off the water.

Rinse the salt pork and slash the rind several times before adding to the beans.

Dice one onion and add to the beans.

Stick the cloves in the remaining onion and add to the beans with mace, cayenne pepper and diced carrots.

Pour in **4 L (16 c)** of water, cover and simmer for 3 hours or until the beans are very tender.

Remove the piece of salt pork.

Pour soup into the blender and purée.

Return soup to your soup pot, adding thinly sliced beef and bring to the boil.

Remove from heat and stir in the sherry just before serving.

Garnish with slices of egg and lemon.

Apple and Lemon
Serves 8

8 Mackintosh or Spy apples, peeled, cored and puréed in the blender
120 ml (1/2 c) lemon juice
240 ml (1 c) sour cream
720 ml (3 c) 18% cream
15 ml (1 tbsp) curry powder
120 ml (1/2 c) Calvados
120 ml (1/2 c) white chocolate chips
30 ml (2 tbsp) chopped fresh mint

Put all ingredients in a large mixing bowl and whisk together well.

Let stand in the fridge, covered, for 8 hours.

Whisk well before serving.

Oyster Bisque
Serves 4

1 L (4 c) fresh oysters
720 ml (3 c) chicken stock
120 ml (1/2 c) fine bread crumbs
80 ml (1/3 c) finely chopped onion
240 ml (1 c) finely diced celery
1 L (4 c) milk, scalded
30 ml (2 tbsp) butter
60 ml (1/4 c) sherry

Drain the oysters and reserve the liquid.

Put chicken stock in your soup pot, add the reserved oyster liquid, bread crumbs, onion, and celery.

Boil slowly, stirring frequently for about 30 minutes.

Process in the blender until onion and celery are puréed – then return to the soup pot.

Stir in the milk, butter and sherry and heat through.

Drop an even number of oysters into each soup bowl, drowning in hot soup just before serving.

Blackberry and Cantaloupe with Smoked Salmon
Serves 6 – 8

240 ml (1 c) purée of blackberries
480 ml (2 c) peeled, seeded puréed
   cantaloupe
180 g (6 oz) julienne of smoked
   salmon
240 ml (1 c) ricotta cheese
240 ml (1 c) sour cream
15 ml (1 tbsp) chopped fresh dill
120 ml (1/2 c) blackberry jam
240 ml (1 c) blackberry wine
30 ml (2 tbsp) orange zest
1 1/2 L (6 c) 18% cream

Place all ingredients in a mixing bowl and whisk well.

Let stand for 8 hours in the fridge, covered.

Whisk again before serving.

Curried Onion
Serves 8 – 10

60 ml (1/4 c) olive oil
240 ml (1 c) diced Spanish onion
240 ml (1 c) diced red onion
240 ml (1 c) diced green onions
240 ml (1 c) peeled onions
30 ml (2 tbsp) diced garlic
30 ml (2 tbsp) mango chutney
60 ml (1/4 c) curry powder
2 L (8 c) veal velouté

Put oil into your soup pot on stove at high heat.

When oil gets hot add all onions and cook on high for 6 minutes, while stirring constantly.

Add garlic and cook until garlic starts to turn brown.

Add chutney and curry then cook for 1 minute while stirring.

Add velouté, and bring back briefly to the boil.

Tomato, Ham and Basil
Serves 6 – 8

460 g (1 lb) ham diced into
   1/2 cm (1/4 in) pieces
1 1/2 L (6 c) peeled seeded diced
   tomatoes
120 ml (1/2 c) diced onions
120 ml (1/2 c) diced green pepper
240 ml (1 c) chopped fresh basil
15 ml (1 tbsp) diced garlic
240 ml (1 c) tomato purée

Put all ingredients in a heavy soup pot on high heat and bring to the boil.

Reduce heat and simmer for 20 minutes.

Bring back to the boil before serving.

Cream of B.B.Q. Chicken
Serves 6

1 L (4 c) chicken stock
480 ml (2 c) finely chopped celery
1 small clove of garlic pressed
180 ml (3/4 c) 35% cream
480 ml (2 c) minced cooked B.B.Q. chicken
120 ml (1/2 c) finely grated Parmesan cheese

Put stock in a large soup pot and bring to the boil.

Add the celery and garlic and simmer for 10 minutes or until tender.

Pour into a blender and purée – then return to the soup pot.

Add the cream and bring to the boiling point.

Stir in the chicken and cheese and heat, stirring until the cheese is melted, and the soup is well blended.

Jerusalem Artichoke
Serves 4

460 g (1 lb) Jerusalem artichokes
600 ml (2 1/2 c) chicken stock
30 ml (2 tbsp) butter
30 ml (2 tbsp) all-purpose flour
600 ml (2 1/2 c) milk
80 ml (1/3 c) freshly grated Parmesan cheese

After steaming the artichokes, allow them to cool before removing the skins with the tip of a sharp knife.

Combine the artichokes and **180 ml (3/4 c)** of the stock in blender and purée.

Melt butter in a small pan and stir in the flour quickly – cook stirring until smooth and bubbly.

Stir in the milk slowly and cook stirring constantly until slightly thickened.

In your soup pot combine the milk mixture, puréed artichokes and remaining stock.

Cook over low heat, stirring occasionally, for about 5 minutes.

Stir in the cheese just before serving.

Chilled Parsnip

Serves 10

1 L (4 c) cooked, puréed parsnips
480 ml (2 c) sour cream
1 large roasted red pimento pepper,
   puréed
120 ml (1/2 c) roasted onion, puréed
3 cloves roasted garlic, puréed
60 ml (2 fl oz) balsamic vinegar
15 ml (1 tbsp) diced fresh sage
30 ml (2 tbsp) salt
30 ml (2 tbsp) brown sugar
480 ml (2 c) 18% cream
120 ml (1/2 c) grated Stilton cheese

Put all ingredients in a large bowl and whisk well, making sure the cheese has dissolved.

Place in the fridge and let stand for 2 hours.

Mix again and serve.

Orange Ruffy with Mandarin Orange

Serves 6

720 ml (3 c) fish stock
680 g (1 1/2 lbs) orange ruffy fillets,
   cut into 1 cm (1/2 in) pieces
60 g (2 oz) orange zest – julienne
60 g (2 oz) lemon zest – julienne
240 ml (1 c) white of leek, diced
12 mandarin oranges peeled,

seeded, chopped
4 strands of saffron
30 g (1 oz) lemon juice
30 g (1 oz) chopped chervil
30 g (1 oz) chopped dill

Put all ingredients in a pot on high heat and bring to the boil.

Boil for 3 minutes.

Remove from stove and serve.

Beef Stroganoff

Serves 10

60 ml (1/4 c) vegetable oil
680 g (1 1/2 lbs) tenderloin tips,
   into 1 cm (1/2 in) pieces
30 small mushroom caps
30 peeled pearl onions
3 cloves garlic, chopped
240 ml (1 c) red wine
5 ml (1 tsp) diced tarragon
30 ml (2 tbsp) tomato paste
2 L (8 c) demi-glace
240 ml (1 c) sour cream

Put oil in a heavy soup pot – heat on high.

When oil just begins to smoke, add beef and brown well on all sides.

Remove beef from heat and set aside.

Still on high, add mushrooms and onions to the oil and cook for 5 minutes.

Then add garlic and cook until brown.

Add wine, tarragon and tomato paste and reduce by half.

Add demi-glace and bring back to the boil.

Return beef and whatever renderings it has produced.

Add sour cream.

Turn off and let stand for 3 minutes before serving.

Note: Beef will be, and should be, rare.

Pearl Onion
Serves 8

460 g (1 lb) pearl onions*
1 clove garlic, diced
240 ml (1 c) dry white wine
1 1/2 L (6 c) chicken stock
2 bay leaves
30 ml (2 tbsp) tomato paste
120 ml (1/2 c) Limburger cheese, shredded

(If you have ever attempted to peel pearl onions, you will be pleased to know that frozen packs are available in most supermarkets and ideal for this and other recipes in this book that include pearl onions.)

In a medium-sized soup pot, put onion, garlic, wine, stock, bay leaves and tomato paste.

Bring to the boil on high heat.

Boil for 5 minutes, then whisk in cheese until completely melted.

Antipasto
Serves 6 – 8

120 ml (1/2 c) julienne Genoa salami
120 ml (1/2 c) julienne prosciutto
120 ml (1/2 c) julienne Calabria salami
120 ml (1/2 c) sliced pepperoni
60 ml (1/4 c) pitted black olives
60 ml (1/4 c) pitted green olives
115 g (1/4 lb) baby eggplant
1 1/4 L (5 c) peeled, seeded, chopped tomatoes
15 ml (1 tbsp) chopped oregano
4 whole cloves of garlic
20 whole, peeled pearl onions (frozen packs of these come perfectly peeled and sized)
240 ml (1 c) extra virgin olive oil
120 ml (1/2 c) diced fennel
60 ml (1/4 c) Provolone cheese grated

Put all ingredients, except cheese, into a heavy soup pot on high heat and bring to a boil.

Lower heat and simmer covered for 20 minutes.

Bring back to the boil and whisk in cheese until completely melted.

Duck Florentine
Serves 8 – 10

60 ml (1/4 c) butter
460 g (1 lb) boned, skinned raw duck
    meat – 1 cm (1/2 in) slices
240 ml (1 c) peeled pearl onions
460 g (1 lb) spinach, stemmed,
    washed and chopped
240 ml (1 c) white of leek, julienne
60 ml (1/4 c) julienne fresh
    chanterelles
60 ml (1/4 c) raw wild rice
30 ml (2 tbsp) fresh chopped
    rosemary
30 ml (2 tbsp) julienne of sun-dried
    tomato
240 ml (1 c) sweet vermouth
15 ml (1 tbsp) roasted garlic chopped
60 ml (1/4 c) roasted red pepper
    julienne
1 1/2 L (6 c) duck stock – dark
60 ml (1/4 c) shredded Tuscanello
    cheese
120 ml (1/2 c) maraschino cherries

Melt butter in your soup pot on
high heat.

When butter has melted, add
duck and cook for 8 minutes.

Add onions, spinach, leek,
mushrooms, rice, rosemary and
sun-dried tomatoes and cook for
5 minutes while stirring well.

Add vermouth, garlic, peppers, and
stock and bring back to the boil.

Whisk in cheese until completely
melted.

Add cherries.

Cream of Carrot
Serves 4

480 ml (2 c) carrots chopped
1 medium onion, quartered
360 ml (1 1/2 c) milk
240 ml (1 c) chicken stock
120 ml (1/2 c) butter
120 ml (1/2 c) water
2 whole cloves
30 ml (2 tbsp) flour
120 ml (1/2 c) 35% cream

Put carrots, onion, milk and
chicken stock into a blender and
process 1 cycle at liquefy.

Drain through colander, reserving
liquid.

Sauté vegetables in butter, add
water and cloves and cook until
tender.

Remove cloves.

Pour half the reserved liquid, the
vegetables, butter and flour into
blender, cover, and process at
blend until smooth.

Pour into saucepean, add
remaining liquid and cook slowly
for about 10 minutes, stirring
constantly.

Stir in cream just before serving.

Caribou Stew
Serves 10 – 12

60 ml (1/4 c) oil
680 g (1 1/2 lbs) ground caribou
30 ml (2 tbsp) chopped garlic
240 ml (1 c) diced onion
120 ml (1/2 c) diced carrots
120 ml (1/2 c) diced green pepper
120 ml (1/2 c) diced turnip
240 ml (1 c) diced leek
120 ml (1/2 c) diced potato
230 g (1/2 lb) double-smoked bacon
   cut into **1/2 cm (1/4 in)** pieces
60 ml (1/4 c) chili sauce
15 ml (1 tbsp) chopped thyme
15 ml (1 tbsp) chopped rosemary
30 ml (2 tbsp) red currant jelly
30 ml (2 tbsp) tomato paste
45 ml (3 tbsp) raw long grain rice
2 L (8 c) beef stock

Cook caribou in oil, while stirring, until brown.

Add garlic and all of the vegetables and cook another 5 minutes on high, while stirring.

Add all other ingredients and bring to the boil.

Reduce heat and simmer for 20 minutes, covered.

Almond
Serves 4

240 ml (1 c) blanched almonds,
   finely ground
720 ml (3 c) chicken stock
1 small onion, stuck with one clove
1/2 bay leaf
75 ml (5 tbsp) butter
30 ml (2 tbsp) flour
120 ml (1/2 c) hot milk
240 ml (1 c) 35% cream
Slivered toasted almonds for garnish

Into your soup pot put ground almonds, chicken stock, onion and bay leaf.

Simmer covered for 30 minutes.

Discard onion and bay leaf.

In a saucepan melt butter, stir in flour, then gradually stir in milk.

Cook over low heat stirring constantly, until smooth and thickened.

Add mixture to your soup pot.

Cook over slow heat, stirring constantly for 5 minutes.

Remove from heat and stir in the cream.

Heat through once more, but do not permit to boil.

Serve garnished with sprinkles of slivered toasted almonds.

Wild Turkey Gumbo
Serves 6 – 8

60 ml (1/4 c) vegetable oil
900 g (2 lbs) wild turkey breast – raw
   – cut into 1 cm (1/2 in) pieces
240 ml (1 c) sliced onion
240 ml (1 c) sliced red pepper
120 ml (1/2 c) sliced green pepper
120 ml (1/2 c) diced carrots
120 ml (1/2 c) diced celery
120 ml (1/2 c) cleaned sliced okra
4 cloves garlic
1 L (4 c) peeled, seeded diced
   tomatoes
30 ml (2 tbsp) coriander
1 anise star
1/4 stick of cinnamon
30 g (1 oz) Spanish paprika
120 ml (1/2 c) chili sauce
30 ml (1 fl oz) lemon juice
480 ml (2 c) turkey or chicken stock
60 ml (1/4 c) raw long grain rice

Heat oil in your soup pot on
high heat.

When the oil is hot, add the
turkey and stir-fry for 8 minutes.

Add all other ingredients, and
bring to the boil.

Turn heat down, cover, and
simmer for 40 minutes.

Bring back to the boil before
serving.

Vichyssoise #1
Serves 4

480 ml (2 c) chicken stock
480 ml (2 c) cubed potatoes
60 ml (1/4 c) leek chopped
240 ml (1 c) milk
240 ml (1 c) 35% cream
Chives for garnish

Put stock, cubed potatoes and
leek into a blender, cover and
process 2 cycles at liquefy.

Pour into your soup pot and
cook 4 to 5 minutes on medium
heat.

Put remaining ingredients,
except cream and chives, into
the blender and add cooked
mixture.

Cover and process at liquefy
until smooth.

Pour into mixing bowl and stir
in cream.

Chill for 4-6 hours.

Garnish with chopped chives.

Vichyssoise #2
Serves 6

2 medium leeks
60 ml (1/4 c) butter
3 medium potatoes, peeled and
   thinly sliced
1 L (4 c) chicken stock
240 ml (1 c) 35% cream
Fresh chives for garnish

Remove and discard root ends
and dark green parts of the leeks,
thinly slice leeks.

Melt butter in a large soup pot
and add the leeks.

Cook gently for 7 to 10 minutes,
stirring often, until softened but
not colored.

Add potatoes.

Add the stock and bring to
the boil.

Cover and simmer, stirring
occasionally, for 30 minutes.

Process the soup in a blender,
then force through a strainer into
a clean pot.

Add cream, return to the boil,
then chill for 4 to 6 hours.

Serve garnished with chopped
chives.

Ocean Chowder
Serves 12

2 1/2 L (10 c) fish stock
6 strands of saffron
60 ml (1/4 c) peeled chopped
   shallots
1 clove of garlic, diced
240 ml (1 c) diced leek
230 g (1/2 lb) de-boned and skinned
   mackerel cut into **1 cm (1/2 in)**
   pieces
230 g (1/2 lb) de-boned and
   skinned monkfish cut into
   1 cm (1/2 in) pieces
230 g (1/2 lb) de-boned and skinned
   grouper cut into
   1 cm (1/2 in) pieces
230 g (1/2 lb) smoked eel cut into
   1 cm (1/2 in) pieces
230 g (1/2 lb) de-boned skinned
   marlin cut into **1 cm (1/2 in)**
   pieces
60 ml (1/4 c) cooked long grain rice

Put stock, saffron, shallots, garlic
and leeks into your soup pot and
bring to the boil on high heat.

When it reaches a rolling boil,
add fish and rice. Cover, still
on high, bring back to the boil.

Boil for 3 minutes before serving.

Caviar in Cream
Serves 4

240 ml (1 c) sour cream
12 oysters – shucked – with juice
2 strands of saffron
60 ml (2 oz) lemon juice
15 ml (1 tbsp) zest of lemon – julienne
90 ml (3 fl oz) fine gin
1 L (4 c) 18% cream
5 ml (1 tsp) fresh chopped sorrel
115 g (4 oz) beluga caviar

Put all ingredients, except caviar, in a bowl and stir carefully to fold oysters into soup.

Fold in caviar with a large spoon.

Let stand in the fridge for 8 hours.

Mix with a large wooden spoon before serving.

Shrimp
with Garlic
Serves 8 – 10

230 g (1/2 lb) butter
900 g (2 lbs) peeled de-veined
    shrimp – (**30–35**)
60 ml (1/4 c) diced garlic
120 ml (1/2 c) finely diced onions
2 L (8 c) fish stock
30 ml (2 tbsp) fresh lemon juice
3 strands of saffron

1 bay leaf
30 ml (2 tbsp) chopped parsley

Melt butter in your soup pot on high.

When butter is melted, add the shrimp, garlic and onion and cook, while stirring, until the garlic turns brown.

Add stock, lemon juice, saffron and bay leaf.

Bring to the boil.

Add parsley and serve.

Sour Vegetable
Serves 10

240 ml (1 c) diced onion
120 ml (1/2 c) diced carrots
120 ml (1/2 c) diced celery
120 ml (1/2 c) diced green pepper
120 ml (1/2 c) diced turnip
120 ml (1/2 c) diced fennel
120 ml (1/2 c) diced parsnips
480 ml (2 c) diced tomatoes
240 ml (1 c) sauerkraut
1 1/4 L (5 c) vegetable stock
60 ml (1/4 c) cooked long grain rice

Put all ingredients into your soup pot.

Bring to the boil on high heat.

Reduce heat and simmer uncovered for 30 minutes.

Rabbit and Prune
Serves 8

460 g (1 lb) cooked rabbit meat cut
    into 1 cm (1/2 in) pieces
240 ml (1 c) pitted, sliced prunes
240 ml (1 c) prune juice
115 g (4 oz) dried chanterelle
    mushrooms
120 ml (1/2 c) Port wine
1 1/2 L (6 c) velouté

Place all ingredients into your
soup pot and bring to the boil
on high heat.

Reduce heat and simmer for
10 minutes.

Leek and Bean
Serves 8

240 ml (1 c) dried navy beans,
    soaked overnight
240 ml (1 c) diced leek
2 3/4 L (11 c) vegetable stock
15 ml (1 tbsp) diced garlic
60 ml (1/4 c) chopped basil
60 ml (1/4 c) chervil
15 ml (1 tbsp) diced oregano
15 ml (1 tbsp) diced thyme
15 ml (1 tbsp) diced sage
15 ml (1 tbsp) diced rosemary

Place drained beans, leek, stock
and garlic in your soup pot on
high heat and bring to the boil.

Reduce heat and simmer
uncovered for 2 hours, or until
beans are soft.

Add the herbs and bring to
the boil.

Boil for 3 minutes.

Red Wine
Serves 8

45 ml (3 tbsp) clarified butter
240 ml (1 c) onion, finely diced
15 ml (1 tbsp) diced garlic
60 ml (1/4 c) Merlot
60 ml (1/4 c) Burgundy
60 ml (1/4 c) sherry
240 ml (1 c) Chianti
90 g (3 oz) dried morels
1 1/2 L (6 c) demi-glace

Put butter in a heavy soup pot
on high heat.

When butter becomes hot, add
onion and cook for 2 minutes
while stirring.

Add garlic and cook until golden
brown.

Add wine and morels, and reduce
by half.

Add demi-glace, bring to the boil
before serving.

Old Fashioned Chicken and Rice
Serves 12

680 g (1 1/2 lbs) raw chicken meat cut into **1 cm (1/2 in)** pieces
120 ml (1/2 c) diced onion
120 ml (1/2 c) diced leeks
120 ml (1/2 c) diced celery
2 cloves of garlic crushed
60 ml (1/4 c) diced green pepper
60 ml (1/4 c) raw long grain rice
2 L (8 c) chicken stock
30 ml (2 tbsp) chopped parsley

Place all ingredients into your soup pot.

Bring to the boil and boil for 5 minutes.

Reduce heat and simmer uncovered for 30 minutes.

Seafood Supreme
Serves 6 – 8

45 ml (3 tbsp) olive oil
2 cloves garlic minced
1 leek stalk chopped
1 red pepper sliced
240 ml (1 c) English cucumber, julienne – **5 cm (2 in)** strips
480 ml (2 c) mushrooms, sliced
120 ml (1/2 c) white wine

1 L (4 c) fish or chicken stock
15 ml (1 tbsp) chopped fresh dill
15 ml (1 tbsp) capers
230 g (1/2 lb) mussels cleaned
230 g (1/2 lb) clams cleaned
12 large shrimp peeled and de-veined
12 sea scallops
2 limes quartered

Heat oil in a large deep pan over medium-high heat.

Add garlic, leek, red pepper, cucumber and mushrooms and cook for about 5 minutes, stirring occasionally.

Add wine, stock, dill, and capers and bring to a boil.

Add mussels, clams and shrimp and cook just until clams and mussels have opened.

Add scallops, poach 2 minutes in the soup.

Serve garnished with lime quarters on edge of each bowl.

Abalone Chowder
Serves 4

4 slices bacon diced
6 slices abalone, pounded thin and diced
1 medium potato diced
1 medium onion minced
360 ml (1 1/2 c) hot water
720 ml (3 c) light cream, heated
15 ml (1 tbsp) butter

Cook bacon until golden in a medium soup pot.

Drain off all but **30 ml (2 tbsp)** of fat from pan.

Add abalone, potato and onion and sauté until golden brown.

Add hot water and simmer until abalone and potatoes are tender.

Add heated cream and butter and blend thoroughly.

Season to taste.

Serve very hot.

Irish Nectar
Serves 12

60 ml (1/4 c) oil
680 g (1 1/2 lbs) ground mutton
240 ml (1 c) diced onions
240 ml (1 c) diced potatoes
240 ml (1 c) diced parsnip
120 ml (1/2 c) diced carrots
15 ml (1 tbsp) diced garlic
60 ml (1/4 c) tomato paste
15 ml (1 tbsp) curry powder
45 ml (3 tbsp) sticky rice
2 1/4 L (9 c) beef stock

In a heavy soup pot brown mutton in oil on high heat.

Add all the other ingredients and bring to a boil.

Reduce heat and simmer for 40 minutes.

Hopped-Up Hamburger
Serves 6

60 ml (1/4 c) oil
680 g (1 1/2 lbs) ground beef
240 ml (1 c) diced onions
240 ml (1 c) diced green pepper
120 ml (1/2 c) diced celery
30 ml (2 tbsp) diced garlic
240 ml (1 c) chili sauce
120 ml (1/2 c) tomato paste
1 L (4 c) beef stock
5 ml (1 tsp) diced oregano
240 ml (1 c) cooked elbow
  macaroni

Put oil in your soup pot and take to high heat.

When oil gets hot add beef and cook until brown while stirring.

Then add onion, green pepper, celery and garlic and cook for another 5 minutes.

Add the chili sauce, tomato paste, beef stock and oregano and bring to the boil.

Boil for 3 minutes, then add the macaroni.

Coq au Vin
Serves 6 – 8

60 g (2 oz) porcini mushrooms
80 ml (1/3 c) clarified butter
1 – 1 1/2 kg (3 lbs) chicken (cut into
  8 pieces)
80 ml (1/3 c) flour
20 peeled pearl onions
10 medium mushrooms quartered
115 g (1/4 lb) double-smoked bacon,
  coarsely chopped
2 cloves garlic minced
1/2 green pepper, coarsely chopped
5 ml (1 tsp) chopped fresh thyme
240 ml (1 c) red Bordeaux wine
30 ml (2 tbsp) tomato paste
1 L (4 c) chicken stock
15 ml (1 tbsp) red currant jelly
5 ml (1 tsp) chopped fresh tarragon

Soak porcini mushrooms in
480 ml (2 c) warm water for
15 minutes.

Heat half the butter in a deep
ovenproof pan, dredge chicken
in flour and brown well on all
sides in hot butter.

Remove chicken and set aside.

Add remaining butter to pan –
add onions, drained porcini
mushrooms, quartered
mushrooms, bacon, garlic,
green pepper and thyme.

Deglaze pan with wine.

Whisk in tomato paste, then
chicken stock and bring to
the boil.

Add red currant jelly and
tarragon and mix well.

Return chicken to pan, cover
and cook in a preheated 180° C
(350° F) oven for 25 minutes.

Remove cover and continue
cooking for an additional
50 minutes or until chicken
is tender.

Snails Fond Brun
Serves 6

30 ml (1 fl oz) olive oil
240 ml (1 c) diced shallots
6 cloves of garlic, diced
6 cans of snails – drained and rinsed
240 ml (1 c) dry red wine
180 g (6 oz) dried cep mushrooms
60 ml (1/4 c) tomato paste
480 ml (2 c) beef stock
720 ml (3 c) demi-glace

Heat oil in a heavy soup pot on
high heat.

When oil is hot, add shallots and
cook while stirring for 2 minutes.

Add garlic and cook until brown.

Add snails, wine and mushrooms
– reduce by half.

Add tomato paste and stock and
bring to the boil.

Stir in demi-glace.

Bring back to the boil before serving.

B.B.Q. Shark in Broth
Serves 8 – 10

900 g (2 lbs) shark fillets, boned, skinned and cut into **1 cm (1/2 in)** pieces
2 L (8 c) fish or chicken stock
240 ml (1 c) diced onion
240 ml (1 c) diced leek
30 ml (2 tbsp) diced garlic
1 anise star
3 strands of saffron
120 ml (1/2 c) roasted red peppers, chopped
120 ml (1/2 c) cooked wild rice
120 ml (1/2 c) shredded, 6-year-old white cheddar

B.B.Q. shark for 2 minutes on each side.

Remove and cool.

Into your soup pot add stock, onion, leek, garlic, anise star, saffron and red pepper.

Bring to the boil on high heat.

Add shark and rice.

Bring back to the boil again.

Whisk in cheese and keep whisking until cheese is completely melted.

McCartney's Vegetable Stew
Serves 12 – 14

2 3/4 L (11 c) vegetable stock
240 ml (1 c) diced onions
240 ml (1 c) diced leek
1 jalapeno pepper diced
120 ml (1/2 c) turnip diced
120 ml (1/2 c) parsnip diced
120 ml (1/2 c) diced celery
60 ml (1/4 c) diced fennel
60 ml (1/4 c) diced carrots
60 ml (1/4 c) chili sauce
60 ml (1/4 c) butternut squash chopped
120 ml (1/2 c) red lentils
1 L (4 c) peeled, seeded chopped tomatoes
15 ml (1 tbsp) chopped oregano
60 g (2 oz) chopped black truffle
30 ml (2 tbsp) roasted garlic chopped
30 ml (2 tbsp) fresh chopped rosemary

Put all ingredients in a large soup pot on high heat, and bring to the boil.

Reduce heat and simmer for 60 minutes, stirring occasionally.

Bring back to the boil just before serving.

Black Forest Mushroom with Asparagus
Serves 8 – 10

After cutting away approximately half the tough stem on each, soak **180 g (6 oz)** of dried Black Forest mushrooms in water in a bowl at room temperature for 2 hours, the water just covering them.

Slice the mushrooms.

Reserve the water in which you soaked the mushrooms.

2 L (8 c) chicken stock
240 ml (1 c) sliced onions
240 ml (1 c) sliced green pepper
15 ml (1 tbsp) sliced garlic
15 ml (1 tbsp) julienne of fresh
 ginger
2 bunches of watercress, chopped
 into **6** equal portions
60 ml (1/4 c) "whitewash"
 (equal parts cornstarch and water)
60 ml (1/4 c) Hoisin sauce

Put stock and mushroom water into your soup pot on high heat and bring to the boil.

Add onions, peppers, garlic, ginger and watercress to the stock.

Bring back to the boil.

Whisk in "whitewash," and once it is thick whisk in Hoisin sauce.

Soup is ready to serve.

Chicken Mango
Serves 8 – 10

60 ml (1/4 c) butter
680 g (1 1/2 lbs) diced chicken,
 1 cm (1/2 in) pieces
2 diced Scotch bonnet peppers
30 ml (2 tbsp) diced garlic
Juice from **1** lemon
480 ml (2 c) shredded mango flesh
240 ml (1 c) chicken stock
120 ml (1/2 c) coconut milk
60 ml (1/4 c) dark brown sugar
60 ml (1/4 c) chopped coriander
1 1/2 L (6 c) chicken velouté

Melt butter on high heat in your soup pot and add chicken, Scotch bonnets and garlic.

Cook while stirring for 4 to 5 minutes.

Add lemon juice, mango, stock, coconut milk and bring to the boil.

Add sugar and coriander.

Whisk in the velouté.

Bring back to the boil and serve.

Beef and Clam Stew
Serves 10 – 12

60 ml (1/4 c) vegetable oil
680 g (1 1/2 lbs) inside round steak, diced **1 cm (1/2 in)** pieces
240 ml (1 c) diced onions
240 ml (1 c) diced mushrooms
120 ml (1/2 c) fine diced carrots
120 ml (1/2 c) diced leeks
120 ml (1/2 c) diced green pepper
60 ml (1/4 c) diced turnip
60 g (2 oz) dried porcini mushrooms
115 g (1/4 lb) raw bacon, diced
120 ml (1/2 c) red wine
120 ml (1/2 c) tomato paste
2 L (8 c) beef stock
32 little neck clams, cleaned with shells

On high heat, brown beef on all sides in oil in a heavy soup pot.

Then add all the vegetables, plus the bacon and cook for 3 to 4 minutes while stirring.

Add wine and tomato paste and reduce by 1/3.

Add the stock and bring back to the boil.

Reduce heat and simmer for 15 minutes.

Drop clams into soup and continue to simmer until clams open.

Serve an equal number of clams in each bowl.

Macaroni and Beans in Tomato
Serves 8

2 L (8 c) seeded, peeled, chopped tomatoes
480 ml (2 c) chicken or vegetable stock
60 ml (1/4 c) white navy beans, raw
240 ml (1 c) diced onion
120 ml (1/2 c) diced green pepper
30 ml (2 tbsp) chopped garlic
60 ml (1/4 c) chopped basil
240 ml (1 c) cooked elbow macaroni

Put tomatoes, stock and beans into your soup pot and bring to the boil on high heat.

Reduce heat and simmer for 50 minutes, covered.

Add onion, green pepper, garlic and basil and bring back to the boil. (Add more stock if it becomes too thick.)

Boil for 5 minutes.

Add the macaroni before serving.

Roasted Garlic Mornay
Serves 8

60 ml (1/4 c) clarified butter
240 ml (1 c) fresh sliced garlic
120 ml (1/2 c) fine diced onion
480 ml (1 pint) stout
1 1/2 L (6 c) chicken velouté
240 ml (1 c) shredded Swiss cheese
60 ml (1/4 c) grated Parmesan
cheese

Place butter, garlic and onion into a medium-sized pot.

Cook on high heat until the onion and garlic turn dark brown, stirring constantly.

Add beer and bring to the boil.

Still on high heat, add velouté and keep stirring.

Bring to a boil and whisk in cheeses until completely melted.

Stinky
Serves 6

60 ml (1/4 c) shredded Limburger
cheese
115 g (1/4 lb) shredded Stilton cheese
115 g (1/4 lb) shredded Gorgonzola
cheese
120 ml (1/2 c) grated Romano
240 ml (1 c) diced onion

240 ml (1 c) vegetable stock
1 L (4 c) béchamel
120 ml (1/2 c) 35% cream

Put cheeses, onion, and vegetable stock in a pot on medium-high heat.

Whisk until cheeses are completely melted.

Then add béchamel and bring to the boil, slowly.

Add cream, and bring to the boil slowly.

Ham and Mustard
Serves 8

240 ml (1 c) dry white wine
240 ml (1 c) ham stock
480 ml (2 c) diced ham –
1/2 cm (1/4 in) pieces
120 ml (1/2 c) chopped bread and
butter pickles
120 ml (1/2 c) diced onion
60 ml (1/4 c) Dijon mustard
15 ml (1 tbsp) chopped capers
1 L (4 c) chicken velouté

Place wine, stock, ham, chopped pickles, onion, mustard and capers into soup pot.

Bring to the boil on high heat.

Reduce heat and simmer until liquid is reduced by 1/3.

Add velouté, and return to a boil.

B.B.Q. Back Ribs in a Bowl
Serves 6

1 1/2 kg (3 lbs) of back ribs (have your butcher remove the bones). Season with salt and pepper and B.B.Q. the meat. Let cool and cut into 1 cm (1/2 in) pieces
240 ml (1 c) diced onion
240 ml (1 c) diced green pepper
720 ml (3 c) B.B.Q. sauce
2 cloves of garlic, minced
5 ml (1 tsp) dried oregano
30 ml (1 fl oz) malt vinegar
30 g (1 oz) brown sugar
720 ml (3 c) tomato juice
240 ml (1 c) strong beef stock

Put all ingredients in your soup pot on medium heat.

Gradually bring to the boil, then simmer covered for 10 minutes.

Crazy Turkey
Serves 8

680 g (1 1/2 lbs) cooked turkey meat
240 ml (1 c) diced onion
240 ml (1 c) diced green pepper
13 chopped jalapeno peppers
1 L (4 c) tomato sauce
480 ml (2 c) turkey stock
15 ml (1 tbsp) chopped coriander

60 ml (1/4 c) cooked long grain rice
5 ml (1 tsp) dried oregano
2 bay leaves

Place all ingredients in your soup pot on medium-high heat and cook for 50 minutes.

Increase heat and bring to a rolling boil.

Remove from heat.

Garnish with nachos and serve.

Old Fashioned Cabbage
Serves 8

4 thick slices of bacon, diced into 1/2 cm (1/4 in) pieces
2 onions, sliced
1 turnip, diced
2 carrots, diced
2 potatoes, cubed
1 small head green cabbage, shredded
1 L (4 c) chicken stock
480 ml (2 c) water
6 parsley sprigs and bay leaf tied together with thread
60 ml (1/4 c) grated Parmesan cheese (for garnish)

Place all ingredients except the cheese into your soup pot.

Simmer partially covered for 1 1/2 to 2 hours.

Discard the parsley/bay bundle.

Serve garnished with the cheese.

Hot and Sour
Serves 8

60 ml (1/4 c) cloud ears (both cloud
ears and golden needles are
found in Chinese specialty stores)
60 ml (1/4 c) golden needles
60 ml (1/4 c) ground pork, shredded
into **3 1/2 cm (1 1/2 in)** long strips
15 ml (1 tbsp) cornstarch
10 ml (2 tsp) sherry
1 L (4 c) chicken stock
15 ml (1 tbsp) soy sauce
2 115-g (4-oz) bean curd cubes,
each cut into **8** pieces
60 ml (4 tbsp) "whitewash"
(equal parts cornstarch and water)
120 ml (1/2 c) water
45 ml (3 tbsp) white wine vinegar
2 ml (1/2 tsp) hot oil
5 ml (1 tsp) sesame seed oil
1 egg, beaten
2 scallions, chopped

Soak cloud ears and needles
in hot water for approximately
15 minutes or until noticeably
increased in size, drain.

Shred cloud ears, cut golden
needles in half.

Mix pork with **15 ml (1 tbsp)**
cornstarch and sherry.

Into a large soup pot pour chicken
stock, soy sauce and bring to the
boil.

Add pork and boil for 1 minute
more.

Add cloud ears, golden needles
and bean curds and boil for
another minute.

Add "whitewash," stir until
thickened – lower heat.

Add water, vinegar and oils and
adjust seasoning to taste.

Slowly stir in egg.

Garnish with scallions.

Sole with Red Grapes
Serves 8 – 10

240 ml (1 c) dry white wine
900 g (2 lbs) sole fillets, diced into
1 cm (1/2 in) pieces
240 ml (1 c) peeled pearl onions
5 ml (1 tsp) diced garlic
240 ml (1 c) sliced mushrooms
15 ml (1 tbsp) Dijon mustard
5 ml (1 tsp) dried tarragon
1 1/2 L (6 c) fish velouté
480 ml (2 c) seedless red grapes

Bring wine, sole, onion, garlic,
mushrooms, mustard and tarragon
to the boil on high heat.

Reduce by boiling until the wine
is almost gone, and the mixture
begins to thicken.

Add velouté and grapes.

Reduce heat to medium and bring
the soup back to the boil, slowly.

When the soup comes to the boil,
it is ready to be served.

German Potato
Serves 6 – 8

2 medium-sized potatoes
1 medium-sized onion
4 stalks celery with green leaves
30 ml (2 tbsp) vegetable oil
1 small bay leaf
30 ml (2 tbsp) butter
480 ml–720 ml (2–3 c) milk
Chopped parsley (for garnish)

Peel and thinly slice potatoes, onion and celery and sauté for 3 to 5 minutes in hot oil.

Place sautéed vegetables into your soup pot, add enough boiling water to cover.

Put bay leaf in pot and boil until vegetables are tender.

Drain vegetables and reserve liquid.

Mash vegetables, whisk back into vegetable stock and add butter.

Thin soup with milk as desired and heat until warm – do not boil.

Egg and Lemon Soup with Meatballs
Serves 8 – 10

460 g (1 lb) lean ground lamb
   or beef
60 ml (1/4 c) raw long grain rice
60 ml (1/4 c) finely chopped onion
30 ml (2 tbsp) finely chopped parsley
1 1/2 L (6 c) chicken stock
480 ml (2 c) water
2 eggs
80 ml (1/3 c) lemon juice
Parsley for garnish

Mix together the meat, rice, onion, parsley and shape into small meatballs using a rounded teaspoon of the meat mixture for each one.

Pour chicken stock and water into your soup pot and bring to the boil.

Add the meatballs.

Reduce heat to simmer and cook, covered, for 20 minutes.

Beat the eggs until thick and lemon in color.

Slowly beat in the lemon juice.

Add **240 ml (1 c)** of the soup broth slowly to the egg and lemon mixture while continuing to beat.

Add the mixture to the soup in the pot and heat through.

Sherry Bisque

Serves 10

1 small ham hock
60 ml (1/4 c) split green peas
1 bay leaf
1 1/2 L (6 c) beef stock
6 slices bacon, diced into
   1/2 cm (1/4 in) bits
60 ml (1/4 c) chopped onion
1 stalk celery, diced
45 ml (3 tbsp) flour
1 230-g (8-oz) can tomato purée
240 ml (1 c) chicken stock
80 ml (1/3 c) sherry
60 ml (1/4 c) butter

Place ham hock, split peas, bay leaf and **1 L (4 c)** of the beef stock into a **4 L (4 qt)** saucepan.

Bring to the boil, reduce heat and simmer.

Sauté bacon in frying pan until the fat is rendered.

Add onion and celery and cook until tender.

Stir in flour and mix to blend.

Add remaining **480 ml (2 c)** of beef stock and cook until slightly thickened.

Add onion mixture to split pea mixture and cook until peas are soft, about 1 1/2 hours.

When done, remove ham hock and bay leaf.

Purée mixture in blender, adding tomato purée, chicken stock and sherry.

Remove bone and skin from ham, adding the lean, diced pork to the purée.

Add butter and stir on medium heat until melted.

Goulash
(The Simple Way)

Serves 8

480 ml (2 c) chopped onion
60 ml (1/4 c) shortening
3 chopped green peppers
45 ml (3 tbsp) tomato paste
460 g (1 lb) lean beef, cut into
   2 1/2 cm (1 in) cubes
dash of red pepper sauce
5 ml (1 tsp) paprika
2 cloves garlic, minced
1 1/2 L (6 c) beef stock
15 ml (1 tbsp) lemon juice
1 ml (1/4 tsp) caraway seeds

In your soup pot cook onion in stortening until transparent.

Add green peppers and tomato paste.

Cover and simmer 10 minutes.

Add meat and remaining ingredients and simmer about 1 1/2 hours, until meat is tender.

Note: People tell me that this

soup is twice as good on the second day.

Egg and Lemon
Serves 6

1 1/2 L (6 c) chicken stock
480 ml (2 c) water
10 ml (2 tsp) dried parsley
80 ml (1/3 c) raw long grain rice
2 eggs
Juice of 1 fresh lemon

Put the chicken stock, water, and parsley into your soup pot and bring to the boil.

Add the rice, cover and cook for 25 minutes.

Meanwhile beat the eggs well.

Slowly add the lemon juice to the eggs while continuing to beat or whisk.

Slowly pour the egg and lemon mixture back into the soup pot while stirring vigorously.

Cook over very low heat for a few minutes stirring constantly until slightly thickened.

Do not boil as the mixture will curdle.

Note: This soup does not reheat well.

Veal Tomato
Serves 10 – 12

240 ml (1 c) extra virgin olive oil
900 g (2 lbs) raw veal meat,
    1 cm (1/2 in) cubes
240 ml (1 c) diced Spanish onion
240 ml (1 c) diced green pepper
3 cloves of garlic, sliced
240 ml (1 c) dry red wine
60 ml (1/4 c) sun-dried tomatoes,
    sliced
60 ml (1/4 c) chopped porcini
    mushrooms
2 1/2 L (10 c) tomatoes, peeled,
    seeded and chopped
60 ml (1/4 c) chopped basil
15 ml (1 tbsp) chopped oregano

Put oil into your soup pot on high heat.

When oil is hot, add veal, onion, green pepper, and cook for 5 minutes while stirring.

Add garlic and cook 2 to 3 minutes more.

Add wine, sun-dried tomatoes and mushrooms, cooking until wine is reduced by one half.

Add tomatoes, basil and oregano and bring to the boil.

Reduce heat and simmer for 40 minutes.

Season to taste and serve.

Carrot and Potato

Serves 8

Delicious hot or cold

30 ml (2 tbsp) butter
2 leeks, white part only, sliced
1 L (4 c) potatoes, cubed
720 ml (3 c) sliced carrots
1 1/2 L (6 c) chicken stock
480 ml (2 c) half-and-half cream
Shredded raw carrot

Melt butter in large saucepan and cook leeks several minutes until tender.

Add potatoes, carrots, and stock and bring to the boil.

Reduce heat and simmer for 30 minutes until vegetables are done.

Carefully purée hot soup in blender.

Return purée to pan.

Add half-and-half cream.

Heat to serving temperature.

Garnish soup with shredded carrot.

Chicken Ball

Serves 8 – 10

Chicken Balls

460 g (1 lb) ground chicken
60 ml (1/4 c) diced onions
5 ml (1 tsp) diced garlic
1 egg
30 ml (2 tbsp) fine bread crumbs
5 ml (1 tsp) fresh sage
5 ml (1 tsp) powdered chicken base

Preheat oven to 190° C (375° F).

Put all ingredients in a mixing bowl – mix well, using your hands.

Grease a baking sheet and start making chicken balls, about **2 1/2 cm (1 in)** in diameter.

Bake for 15 minutes.

Soup

240 ml (1 c) diced onions
240 ml (1 c) diced celery
120 ml (1/2 c) diced carrots
120 ml (1/2 c) diced red peppers
15 ml (1 tbsp) diced garlic
2 L (8 c) chicken stock
30 ml (2 tbsp) chopped parsley

Put all ingredients in your soup pot – on high heat – bring to the boil.

Cook at a rolling boil for 5 minutes.

Add chicken balls.

Bring back to the boil before serving.

Chilled Elderberry
Serves 8

480 ml (2 c) puréed fresh elderberries
240 ml (1 c) elderberry jam
240 ml (1 c) elderberry wine
480 ml (2 c) sour cream
15 ml (1 tbsp) orange zest
120 ml (1/2 c) very small wild blueberries
1 L (4 c) 18% cream
30 ml (1 oz) Cassis liqueur

Put all ingredients in a bowl and whisk well.

Let stand for 8 hours in the fridge.

Whisk well and serve.

White Bean
Serves 6

460 g (1 lb) dried navy beans
1 L (4 c) water
1 smoked ham bone or ham hock
30 ml (2 tbsp) chopped parsley
240 ml (1 c) finely chopped onion
1 clove garlic, minced
480 ml (2 c) finely chopped celery with green tops

Cover beans with water in large pot and soak overnight.

Drain and rinse beans well and return to the pot with ham bone and 3 L (12 c) water.

Simmer, uncovered for 2 hours.

Add parsley, onion, garlic, celery, and simmer uncovered for 1 hour or until vegetables are tender.

Remove ham bone, dice the meat and add meat to the soup.

Spicy Chilled Stilton
Serves 6

240 ml (1 c) shredded Stilton
240 ml (1 c) cream cheese
240 ml (1 c) champagne
1 red Scotch bonnet pepper, minced
5 ml (1 tsp) chopped coriander
120 ml (1/2 c) sour cream
60 ml (1/4 c) buttermilk
720 ml (3 c) 18% cream

Put all ingredients in a blender and purée.

Then let stand in the fridge for 8 hours.

Blend again before serving.

Meatball Soup with Tomatoes

Serves 10

Meatballs

460 g (1 lb) medium ground beef
30 ml (2 tbsp) diced onion
5 ml (1 tsp) diced garlic
1 egg
30 ml (2 tbsp) fine breadcrumbs
5 ml (1 tsp) powdered beef base

Put in a bowl and mix well with your hands, then make **2 1/2 cm (1 in)** round meatballs and place them on a greased baking sheet.

Pre-heat oven to 190° C (375° F) and bake for 10 minutes.

Soup

60 ml (1/4 c) lemon juice
240 ml (1 c) diced onions
240 ml (1 c) diced green pepper
240 ml (1 c) diced carrots
30 ml (2 tbsp) chopped garlic
120 ml (1/2 c) diced leek
2 L (8 c) peeled, seeded, chopped
   tomatoes
5 ml (1 tsp) oregano
5 ml (1 tsp) basil
2 bay leaves
240 ml (1 c) beef stock

Reserve lemon juice and meatballs.

Put all other ingredients in a heavy soup pot on high heat and bring to the boil while stirring.

Reduce heat, cover, and simmer for 35 to 40 minutes more, stirring occasionally.

Stir in meatballs and lemon juice.

Turn up to high and bring back to the boil before serving.

Cream of Sage

Serves 6

60 ml (1/4 c) butter
240 ml (1 c) diced onion
240 ml (1 c) diced leek
5 ml (1 tsp) diced garlic
15 ml (1 tbsp) diced sun-dried
   tomatoes
120 ml (1/2 c) dry white wine
180 ml (3/4 c) chopped fresh sage
5 ml (1 tsp) Dijon mustard
720 ml (3 c) vegetable or chicken
   stock
45 ml (3 tbsp) white roux

Put butter into your soup pot and bring to medium heat.

When butter is melted, add onion and leek and sauté for 3 minutes while stirring.

Add garlic and sun-dried tomatoes and cook another 2 minutes.

Add wine and sage and bring to the boil.

Stir in mustard and stock and bring back to the boil.

Whisk in roux and boil for an additional 2 minutes.

Scampi Soprano
Serves 8

230 g (1/2 lb) butter
900 g (2 lbs) cleaned scampi meat – 1/2 cm (1/4 in) pieces
5 ml (1 tsp) black truffles, julienne
5 ml (1 tsp) white truffles, julienne
240 ml (1 c) hen-in-the-woods mushrooms, sliced
60 ml (1/4 c) peeled and diced shallots
120 ml (1/2 c) very good Madeira wine
15 ml (1 tbsp) chopped fresh marjoram
1 1/2 L (6 c) peeled, seeded, chopped ripe tomatoes
240 ml (1 c) fish stock, or scampi stock made from the shells
115 g (1/4 lb) peeled and shredded Sainte Maure cheese

Put butter in a heavy soup pot on medium-high heat until melted.

Add scampi, truffles and mushrooms as well as the shallots and cook for 4 to 6 minutes more.

Remove scampi and set aside.

Add Madeira and reduce by half.

Add marjoram and tomatoes and cook for 30 minutes.

Add stock, turn to high heat, and boil for 3 to 4 minutes.

Whisk in cheese.

Add scampi.

Vegetable Chili Corn Carne
Serves 12 – 14

240 ml (1 c) fresh corn kernels
240 ml (1 c) diced onion
240 ml (1 c) diced green pepper
240 ml (1 c) diced celery
240 ml (1 c) diced carrots
240 ml (1 c) diced leeks
120 ml (1/2 c) diced eggplant
120 ml (1/2 c) diced zucchini
30 ml (2 tbsp) crushed garlic
120 ml (1/2 c) chili sauce
60 ml (1/4 c) chili powder
1 3-L (100-oz) can plum tomatoes
2 bay leaves
5 ml (1 tsp) thyme
5 ml (1 tsp) oregano
30 ml (2 tbsp) chopped coriander
1 796-ml (28-oz) can red kidney beans

Cook all ingredients for 60 minutes in a large, heavy soup pot over medium-high heat, stirring occasionally.

At end of 60 minutes bring to a boil before serving.

Striped Bass with Basil
Serves 8 – 10

60 ml (1/4 c) butter
900 g (2 lbs) bass fillets − skinned and cubed into **1 cm (1/2 in)** pieces
120 ml (1/2 c) diced onion
120 ml (1/2 c) diced leek
60 ml (1/4 c) diced red pepper
15 ml (1 tbsp) diced garlic
240 ml (1 c) Lager (beer)
720 ml (3 c) chopped, peeled, seeded tomatoes
120 ml (1/2 c) fresh chopped basil
480 ml (2 c) fish stock
60 ml (2 oz) chili sauce
60 ml (1/4 c) cooked wild rice

Put butter and fish in your soup pot, on high heat, and cook for 4 minutes while stirring gently.

Remove the fish and set aside.

Add onion, leeks, pepper and garlic (more butter may be needed) and cook until garlic is brown.

Add beer and reduce by half.

Add tomatoes and basil and let cook for 8 to 10 minutes while stirring.

Add stock and chili sauce and bring to the boil.

Add fish and rice.

Bring back to the boil.

Mulligatawny
Serves 12

60 ml (1/4 c) butter
240 ml (1 c) diced onion
30 ml (2 tbsp) diced garlic
480 ml (2 c) diced leeks
240 ml (1 c) diced carrots
120 ml (1/2 c) diced celery
240 ml (1 c) diced green pepper
120 ml (1/2 c) diced jalapeno pepper
60 ml (1/4 c) basmati rice
120 ml (1/2 c) mango purée
480 ml (2 c) peeled, diced Spy apples
60 ml (1/4 c) curry powder
30 g (1 oz) ginger, julienne
680 g (1 1/2 lbs) double-smoked chicken, **1/2 cm (1/4 in)** cubes
1 3/4 L (7 c) chicken stock
90 ml (6 tbsp) white roux

Put butter in a heavy soup pot on high heat.

When butter has melted, add onion, garlic, leeks, carrots, celery and peppers and cook on high heat for 5 minutes, while stirring.

Add rice, mango, apples, curry powder, and ginger and continue cooking for 1 minute while stirring.

Add chicken and stock and return to the boil.

Reduce heat and simmer for 20 minutes.

Bring back to the boil and whisk in white roux, cooking for another 2 minutes.

Chilled Cucumber with Lox and Oysters
Serves 10

24 shucked oysters, juice reserved
30 ml (2 tbsp) chopped fresh dill
480 ml (2 c) peeled, seeded, purée of cucumber
480 ml (2 c) sour cream
60 g (2 oz) lox, julienne
60 ml (1/4 c) lemon juice
120 ml (1/2 c) sweet vermouth
60 ml (1/4 c) ricotta cheese
1 1/4 L (5 c) 18% cream

Strain oyster juices through cheesecloth to remove any grit.

Put all ingredients including oyster juice into a mixing bowl and whisk.

Let stand in the fridge for 8 hours.

Whisk lightly before serving.

Coquilles St. Jonathyn
Serves 10

120 ml (1/2 c) butter
680 g (1 1/2 lbs) bay scallops
240 ml (1 c) diced onion
3 cloves of garlic diced
240 ml (1 c) sliced chanterelle mushrooms
15 ml (1 tbsp) chopped tarragon
120 ml (1/2 c) dry white wine
1 1/2 L (6 c) fish velouté
60 ml (1/4 c) shredded Swiss cheese
30 ml (2 tbsp) grated Parmesan cheese
240 ml (1 c) 35% cream

Put butter in a heavy soup pot on high heat.

When butter is melted add scallops, onion, garlic, mushrooms and tarragon and cook for 5 minutes, while stirring.

Still on high heat, add wine and reduce by half.

Then add velouté, reducing heat to medium-high and allowing to return to the boil slowly while stirring.

When it has reached the boiling stage, whisk in cheese until completely melted.

Add the cream, bring back to the boil and serve.

Ground Beef with Eggs and Lemon
Serves 12

60 ml (1/4 c) vegetable oil
900 g (2 lbs) ground beef
240 ml (1 c) sliced onion
240 ml (1 c) sliced red pepper
240 ml (1 c) sliced green pepper
15 ml (1 tbsp) sliced garlic
60 ml (1/4 c) white sugar
120 ml (1/2 c) lemon juice
1 1/2 L (6 c) beef stock
4 lemons, cut in half and sliced thin
6 eggs, beaten
45 ml (3 tbsp) "whitewash"
    (equal parts water and cornstarch)
15 ml (1 tbsp) Hoisin sauce

Add oil to a large wok on high heat.

When oil is hot, add beef and cook while stirring, until completely brown.

Then add onion, pepper, garlic and cook on high heat for 2 minutes.

Add sugar, lemon juice and stock.

When the soup starts to come to the boil add the lemon slices.

Bring to the boil and whisk in eggs.

Bring back to the boil and whisk in "whitewash."

Add Hoisin sauce and serve.

Sweet Potato
Serves 8

1 L (4 c) peeled and shredded
    sweet potato flesh
240 ml (1 c) diced onion
120 ml (1/2 c) brown sugar
3 whole cloves
1/2 stick cinnamon
240 ml (1 c) brandy
1 1/2 L (6 c) chicken stock
60 ml (1/4 c) white roux

Put all ingredients except roux into your soup pot.

Place on high heat and bring to the boil.

Slowly whisk in roux.

Reduce heat and simmer for 20 minutes.

Return to high heat and once again bring to the boil for 2 minutes.

Chicken with Wild Rice
Serves 12

60 ml (1/4 c) butter
680 g (1 1/2 lbs) raw chicken,
    diced in **1 cm (1/2 in)** pieces
120 ml (1/2 c) wild rice

240 ml (1 c) diced carrots
240 ml (1 c) diced celery
240 ml (1 c) diced red pepper
240 ml (1 c) diced leeks
30 ml (2 tbsp) diced garlic
60 ml (1/4 c) diced sun-dried
   tomatoes
60 ml (2 oz) dried porcini
   mushrooms, crushed
60 ml (2 oz) chili sauce
2 L (8 c) chicken stock
5 ml (1 tsp) chopped rosemary
5 ml (1 tsp) chopped thyme

Put butter, chicken and rice in a heavy soup pot on high heat and cook chicken and rice for 5 to 6 minutes, while stirring.

Add all other ingredients and bring to the boil.

Reduce heat and simmer covered for 40 minutes, or until the rice opens up.

Beef Oscar
Serves 12

60 ml (1/4 c) butter
480 ml (2 c) chopped fresh white
   asparagus
240 ml (1 c) diced onion
240 ml (1 c) sliced button
   mushrooms
680 g (1 1/2 lbs) sirloin steak cut
   into 1 cm (1/2 in) cubes – grilled
   to rare
240 ml (1 c) snow crab meat

180 g (6 oz) foie gras
120 ml (1/2 c) Madeira wine
30 ml (1 oz) green peppercorns
   in brine
1 1/2 L (6 c) demi-glace

Melt butter in a heavy soup pot on high heat.

Add the asparagus, onion, mushrooms and cook on high for 4 to 5 minutes while stirring.

Add charred beef, including any juices collected during grilling.

Then add crab meat and foie gras and cook for 2 minutes while stirring.

Add the wine and reduce by 1/4.

Add peppercorns, brine and demi-glace.

Bring to the boil and serve.

Butterscotch Ripple
Serves 6

1 L (4 c) butterscotch ice cream
720 ml (3 c) 18% cream
120 ml (1/2 c) Scotch whiskey
15 ml (1 tbsp) vanilla extract
60 ml (1/4 c) bitter chocolate chips

Put all ingredients in a blender, purée for 1 minute and serve.

Lox with Cream and Brandy
Serves 8

460 g (1 lb) julienne of lox
240 ml (1 c) dry vermouth
30 g (1 oz) chopped capers
2 strands of saffron
1 1/2 L (6 c) chicken velouté
120 ml (1/2 c) brandy
120 ml (1/2 c) 35% cream

Put lox and vermouth in a pot on medium-high heat and lightly poach for 3 to 4 minutes.

Add capers and velouté and bring to the boil.

Add saffron and brandy and bring back to the boil.

Add cream before serving.

Pheasant a la King
Serves 12

60 ml (1/4 c) butter
680 g (1 1/2 lbs) raw pheasant meat, diced in **1/2 cm (1/4 in)** pieces
120 ml (1/2 c) diced onion
15 ml (1 tbsp) diced garlic
120 ml (1/2 c) diced green pepper
120 ml (1/2 c) diced leek
120 ml (1/2 c) diced smoked bacon, **1 cm (1/2 in)** pieces
30 small mushroom caps

15 ml (1 tbsp) chopped rosemary
1 1/2 L (6 c) pheasant or chicken stock
60 ml (1/4 c) dry white wine
60 ml (1/4 c) Port wine
60 ml (1/4 c) white roux
60 ml (1/4 c) 35% cream

Put butter in a heavy soup pot on high heat.

Add pheasant meat, onion, garlic pepper, leeks and bacon and cook for 8 to 10 minutes, while stirring.

Add the mushrooms and rosemary and cook for another 2 minutes.

Add stock and wines, bring to the boil.

Reduce heat, cover and simmer for 40 minutes.

Bring back to the boil and whisk in roux.

Add cream, bring back to the boil and serve.

Ocean Harvest
Serves 12

230 g (1/2 lb) butter
900 g (2 lbs) peeled, de-veined shrimp **(30–35)**
120 ml (1/2 c) bay scallops
120 ml (1/2 c) lobster meat, diced into **1 cm (1/2 in)** pieces
240 ml (1 c) diced shark, **1 cm (1/2 in)** pieces
120 ml (1/2 c) diced onion
120 ml (1/2 c) diced green of leek

30 ml (2 tbsp) diced garlic
120 ml (1/2 c) sun-dried raspberries
120 ml (1/2 c) brandy
2 L (8 c) fish stock
3 strands of saffron
15 ml (1 tbsp) Spanish paprika
120 ml (1/2 c) orzo pasta, raw

In a heavy soup pot on high heat, put butter, shrimps, scallops, lobster, shark, onion, leeks and garlic.

Cook while stirring for 6 to 8 minutes.

Add raspberries and brandy and cook for one more minute.

Still on high heat, add stock, saffron and paprika and bring to the boil.

Add orzo pasta and cook for 6 more minutes.

Baby Potatoes in Cheese Broth
Serves 8

40 to 50 new mini potatoes, with skin
240 ml (1 c) diced onion
240 ml (1 c) diced leeks
2 cloves crushed garlic
60 ml (1/4 c) diced smoked bacon, 1/2 cm (1/4 in) pieces
1 3/4 L (7 c) chicken stock
15 ml (1 tbsp) chopped fresh rosemary

240 ml (1 c) shredded old cheddar
120 ml (1/2 c) grated Romano cheese

Put potatoes, onion, leeks, garlic, bacon, stock and rosemary into your soup pot.

Bring to the boil on high heat.

Reduce heat and simmer for 40 minutes.

Bring back to the boil, then whisk in cheeses and serve.

Ham and Eggs
Serves 8

1 1/2 L (6 c) ham or chicken stock
480 ml (2 c) diced ham
115 g (1/4 lb) diced, cooked side bacon
240 ml (1 c) diced onion
15 ml (1 tbsp) diced garlic
120 ml (1/2 c) diced green pepper
60 ml (1/4 c) diced celery
120 ml (1/2 c) vermicelli noodles, broken into **1 cm (1/2 in)** pieces, uncooked
10 eggs, beaten

Put stock in a medium-sized pot and add ham, bacon, onion, garlic, green pepper and celery.

Bring to the boil on high heat, add pasta and boil for 5 minutes.

Whisk in eggs and serve.

Spanish Corn

Serves 10

1 1/2 L (6 c) chicken stock
1 L (4 c) fresh corn kernels, scraped
   from the cob
120 ml (1/2 c) diced onion
120 ml (1/2 c) diced green pepper
2 large jalapeno peppers chopped
   (leave seeds in)
120 ml (1/2 c) diced red pepper
120 ml (1/2 c) diced leeks
2 cloves of fresh garlic, diced
45 ml (3 tbsp) Spanish paprika
60 ml (1/4 c) chili sauce
60 ml (1/4 c) chopped fresh
   coriander
30 ml (2 tbsp) brown sugar

Put all ingredients in a large soup pot on high heat.

Bring to a rolling boil.

Reduce heat to medium and simmer for 20 minutes.

Bring back to the boil and serve.

Smoked Pork

Serves 10 – 12

2 1/2 L (10 c) chicken or pork stock
680 g (1 1/2 lbs) smoked pork
   – cut into 1 cm (1/2 in) pieces
240 ml (1 c) shredded cabbage
240 ml (1 c) sauerkraut

120 ml (1/2 c) diced carrots
60 ml (1/4 c) diced green pepper
240 ml (1 c) red onion, sliced
240 ml (1 c) diced celery
120 ml (1/2 c) diced turnip
120 ml (1/2 c) diced parsnips
2 bay leaves
15 ml (1 tbsp) fresh chopped
   rosemary
4 juniper berries
120 ml (1/2 c) diced potatoes
30 ml (2 tbsp) raw long grain rice

Put all ingredients in a large soup pot on high heat.

Bring to the boil.

Reduce heat and simmer for 30 minutes, covered.

Bring back to the boil before serving.

Greek Mushroom

Serves 8 – 10

60 ml (1/4 c) extra virgin olive oil
1 L (4 c) sliced mushrooms
120 ml (1/2 c) sliced onion
45 ml (3 tbsp) chopped garlic
120 ml (1/2 c) sliced green pepper
60 ml (1/4 c) sliced black olives
2 L (8 c) chicken stock
60 ml (1/4 c) sliced cucumber
120 ml (1/2 c) cooked long grain rice
Juice from 1 lemon

Put oil in a medium-sized soup pot on high heat.

When oil is heated, add mushrooms, onion, garlic, green pepper, olives, and cook on high heat for 5 minutes, while stirring.

Add stock and all other ingredients, bring to the boil and serve.

Pork and Peach
Serves 6

80 ml (1/3 c) clarified butter
680 g (1 1/2 lbs) pork, cubed
720 ml (3 c) peaches, diced, peeled (stone removed)
120 ml (1/2 c) diced onion
120 ml (1/2 c) julienne red pepper
1 clove of garlic, diced
1 whole clove
1 L (4 c) pork stock
30 ml (2 tbsp) brown sugar
60 ml (1/4 c) cooked long grain rice
30 ml (1 oz) Galliano

Melt butter in a heavy soup pot, on high heat.

When butter becomes hot, add the pork and brown on all sides.

Add peaches, onion, pepper, diced garlic as well as the whole clove, and cook for 2 to 3 minutes, while stirring.

Add stock, sugar and rice while still on high heat.

Bring to a boil and boil for 5 minutes.

Stir in Galliano and serve.

Steak and Kidney
Serves 10

60 ml (1/4 c) vegetable oil
460 g (1 lb) sirloin, cubed into 1 cm (1/2 in) pieces
230 g (1/2 lb) blanched, veal kidneys, chopped into 1 cm (1/2 in) pieces
240 ml (1 c) diced onion
60 ml (1/4 c) diced green pepper
120 ml (1/2 c) sliced morel mushrooms
120 ml (1/2 c) diced leeks
15 ml (1 tbsp) chopped garlic
15 ml (1 tbsp) fresh chopped rosemary
2 L (8 c) veal or beef stock
120 ml (1/2 c) tomato paste
80 ml (1/3 c) white roux

Put oil in heavy pot on high heat until oil begins to smoke.

Add beef and brown on all sides.

Add kidneys, onions, green pepper, mushrooms, leeks, garlic and rosemary.

Still on high heat, cook while stirring for 5 to 6 minutes.

Add stock and tomato paste and stir.

Bring to a rolling boil and whisk in roux.

Bring back to the boil and serve.

Indian Chicken
Serves 10

60 ml (1/4 c) oil
900 g (2 lbs) minced chicken
240 ml (1 c) diced onion
240 ml (1 c) diced carrots
240 ml (1 c) diced leeks
30 ml (2 tbsp) diced garlic
120 ml (1/2 c) basmati rice
30 ml (2 tbsp) tandoori powder
1 1/2 L (6 c) chicken stock
5 ml (1 tsp) chopped mint
Juice from **1** lemon

Put oil in soup pot on high heat.

Add chicken and cook for 6 to 8 minutes, while stirring.

Then add all other ingredients, still on high heat, and bring to a boil.

Reduce heat to medium and simmer, covered, for 20 minutes.

Pepperoni
Serves 6

60 ml (1/4 c) olive oil
120 ml (1/2 c) diced onion
120 ml (1/2 c) diced green pepper
30 ml (2 tbsp) chopped garlic
680 g (1 1/2 lbs) pizza pepperoni, chopped into **1/2 cm (1/4 in)** pieces

60 ml (1/4 c) diced pimento olives
1 L (4 c) tomato sauce
240 ml (1 c) tomato juice
60 ml (1/4 c) cooked long grain rice
240 ml (1 c) shredded mozzarella cheese

Put oil in your soup pot on high heat.

Add onion, green pepper, garlic, and sauté on medium heat for 5 minutes.

Add pepperoni, olives, tomato sauce, tomato juice and rice and bring back to the boil and cook for 6 to 8 minutes.

Serve, garnished with the mozzarella cheese.

Venison Stew
Serves 16

60 ml (1/4 c) vegetable oil
900 g (2 lbs) diced venison, cut into **1 cm (1/2 in)** pieces
2 1/2 L (10 c) venison or beef stock
240 ml (1 c) diced onion
240 ml (1 c) sliced mushrooms
1/2 jar red currant jelly
240 ml (1 c) dry red wine
240 ml (1 c) diced leeks
460 g (1 lb) double-smoked bacon, **1 cm (1/2 in)** cubes
120 ml (1/2 c) tomato paste
3 cloves of garlic, crushed
120 ml (1/2 c) pearl barley, raw
2 bay leaves

6 juniper berries
240 ml (1 c) diced carrots
120 ml (1/2 c) diced turnip
30 ml (2 tbsp) fresh chopped thyme
240 ml (1 c) diced potatoes

Put oil in your soup pot on high heat.

When oil is hot, add venison and brown well on all sides for 10 to 12 minutes.

Add stock, bring to a boil, then turn heat down and simmer for 30 minutes.

Add all other ingredients and bring to the boil; turn heat down and simmer for 40 minutes.

Bean Soup with Frankfurters
Serves 6 – 8

460 g (16 oz) cooked navy beans
1 1/2 L (6 c) beef stock
1 carrot, chopped
1 celery stalk, chopped
4 strips bacon, cubed
2 onions, chopped
6 Frankfurters, sliced into
    1 cm (1/2 in) pieces
30 ml (2 tbsp) chopped parsley

In your soup pot bring beans, and beef stock to a boil.

Add carrot and celery and continue cooking for 30 minutes.

In a separate frying pan cook the bacon until transparent, add the onion and cook until golden. Set bacon and onion mixture aside.

Mash soup through a sieve or purée in a food processor.

Return to pot and add the bacon and onion mixture.

Add frankfurters and parsley and reheat about 5 minutes.

Chicken Egg Drop
Serves 8

680 g (1 1/2 lbs) diced raw chicken,
    1 cm (1/2 in) pieces
480 ml (2 c) diced onion
240 ml (1 c) diced leeks
240 ml (1 c) diced carrots
240 ml (1 c) diced tomato
240 ml (1 c) diced celery
120 ml (1/2 c) diced green pepper
240 ml (1 c) sliced mushrooms
60 ml (1/4 c) diced red pepper
1 1/2 L (6 c) chicken stock
120 ml (1/2 c) cooked long grain rice
3 eggs

Put all ingredients in your soup pot, except eggs and rice, set on high heat and bring to the boil.

Reduce heat and simmer covered for 20 minutes.

Return to high heat and add rice.

Whisk eggs into boiling soup.

Smoked Salmon with Stilton
Serves 6

45 ml (3 tbsp) salted butter
120 ml (1/2 c) finely diced onion
1 clove garlic, diced
15 ml (1 tbsp) chopped fresh
  tarragon
480 ml (2 c) dry white wine
460 g (1 lb) diced smoked salmon
15 ml (1 tbsp) green peppercorns in
  brine
720 ml (3 c) fish velouté
240 ml (1 c) shredded Stilton cheese
120 ml (4 oz) 35% cream

Put butter, onion and garlic in
your soup pot on high heat and
brown for 4 to 5 minutes while
stirring.

Add tarragon and cook one more
minute while stirring.

Still on high, add wine and bring
back to the boil, reduce the wine
by half.

Add salmon, peppercorns, velouté
and bring back to the boil, stirring
occasionally.

When the soup has come to
the boil, whisk in cheese until
completely melted.

Add cream and serve.

Potato Leek
Serves 6

115 g (1/4 lb) butter
360 ml (1 1/2 c) diced potatoes,
  1/2 cm (1/4 in) pieces
360 ml (1 1/2 c) diced leeks,
  1/2 cm (1/4 in) pieces
240 ml (1 c) diced onion
15 ml (1 tbsp) crushed garlic
60 ml (1/4 c) diced red pepper
15 ml (1 tbsp) herbs de Provençe
1 L (4 c) strong vegetable stock
45 ml (3 tbsp) white roux
60 ml (1/4 c) 35% cream

Put butter into your soup pot
on high heat and add potatoes,
leeks, onion, garlic and red
pepper.

Cook 5 to 6 minutes while
stirring.

Add herbs de Provençe and stock.

Bring to a boil, turn heat down
and simmer, covered, for 12 to
15 minutes.

Bring back to the boil, whisk
in the roux and add the
35% cream.

Bring back to the boil before
serving.

Marlin
with Brie
Serves 8

120 ml (1/2 c) butter
680 g (1 1/2 lbs) fresh marlin,
  diced 1 cm (1/2 in) pieces
240 ml (1 c) diced onion
15 ml (1 tbsp) minced garlic
60 ml (1/4 c) roasted red pepper,
  julienne
15 ml (1 tbsp) chopped capers
4 threads of saffron
60 ml (1/4 c) bourbon
1 1/2 L (6 c) fish stock
Juice of 1 lemon
230 g (1/2 lb) Brie, cleaned and
  chopped
120 ml (1/2 c) cooked wild rice

Melt butter in a medium-sized
soup pot on high heat.

Add fish, onion, garlic, pepper
and capers.

Stir while cooking on high for
5 to 6 minutes.

Add the saffron and bourbon
while stirring.

Add the stock and lemon juice
and bring to the boil.

Once boiling, whisk in the cheese
until completely melted.

Add wild rice, bring back to the
boil and serve.

Cream of
Artichoke
Serves 10

60 ml (1/4 c) butter
1 1/4 L (5 c) cleaned and peeled
  diced artichokes
240 ml (1 c) diced leek – the green
  part
15 ml (1 tbsp) diced garlic
120 ml (1/2 c) diced roasted
  pimento peppers
15 ml (1 tbsp) lemon zest
Juice from 2 lemons
2 L (8 c) strong chicken stock
  (use some powdered base)
90 ml (6 tbsp) white roux
240 ml (1 c) 35% cream
120 ml (1/2 c) dry vermouth

Put butter in a heavy soup pot
on high heat.

Add artichokes, leeks, garlic
and pepper and cook for
5 minutes while stirring.

Still on high heat, add the zest,
juice and stock and bring back
to the boil and cook for 6 to
8 minutes.

Whisk in the roux, add the cream
and bring back to the boil.

Add the vermouth before serving.

Note: The vermouth is added
last for flavoring so it won't be
boiled away.

Spicy Cream of Coriander
Serves 6

1 L (4 c) strong chicken stock
720 ml (3 c) chopped coriander
240 ml (1 c) diced onion
45 ml (3 tbsp) diced garlic
120 ml (1/2 c) jalapeno peppers
    with seeds, chopped
120 ml (1/2 c) diced red pepper
120 ml (1/2 c) diced green pepper
30 ml (2 tbsp) smoked jalapenos
    chopped
120 ml (1/2 c) chili sauce
Juice from 2 lemons
45–60 ml (3–4 tbsp) white roux

Put all ingredients, except the roux, in your soup pot on high heat.

Bring to the boil uncovered for 5 minutes.

Whisk in the roux.

Return to the boil.

Garnish with nacho chips and serve.

Potato and Ham
Serves 8

720 ml (3 c) diced potatoes,
    1 cm (1/2 in) pieces
480 ml (2 c) diced smoked ham,
    cut into 1/2 cm (1/4 in) pieces

240 ml (1 c) diced onion
240 ml (1 c) sour cream
15 ml (1 tbsp) diced garlic
1 1/2 L (6 c) ham or chicken stock
60 ml (4 tbsp) green split peas
240 ml (1 c) medium cheddar,
    shredded
60 ml (1/4 c) Parmesan cheese

Place all ingredients except cheeses into your soup pot.

Bring to the boil.

Reduce heat and simmer for 20 minutes, covered.

Bring back to the boil, whisking in cheeses until completely melted.

Breakfast
Serves 10

60 ml (1/4 c) oil
460 g (1 lb) uncooked breakfast
    sausage cut into 1 cm (1/2 in)
    pieces
460 g (1 lb) uncooked bacon sliced
    in 1 cm (1/2 in) pieces
240 ml (1 c) diced onion
240 ml (1 c) green pepper, diced
60 ml (1/4 c) red pepper, diced small
1 1/2 L (6 c) chicken stock
240 ml (1 c) diced ham
12 eggs, whisked together

Put sausage, bacon, onion and pepper in oil and cook on high heat while stirring for 6 to 8 minutes until everything is golden brown.

Add stock and ham while still on high heat.

Bring to a rolling boil.

Whisk in eggs.

Great with toast points.

Drunken Raspberry
Serves 8

720 ml (3 c) fresh raspberries, crushed
120 ml (1/2 c) raspberry jam
480 ml (2 c) ricotta cheese
60 ml (1/4 c) brandy
60 ml (1/4 c) sherry
60 ml (1/4 c) light rum
60 ml (1/4 c) dark rum
2 ml (1/2 tsp) ground cinnamon
720 ml (3 c) 18% cream
Zest from **1/2** lemon

Put all ingredients in a large mixing bowl and whisk together.

Then let stand in the fridge for 8 to 12 hours.

Whisk again before serving.

Beef with Tuna and Morels
Serves 10

120 ml (1/2 c) olive oil
460 g (1 lb) sirloin steak cut into 1/2 cm (1/4 in) cubes
460 g (1 lb) fresh tuna cut into 1/2 cm (1/4 in) cubes
240 ml (1 c) diced onions
15 ml (1 tbsp) fresh garlic, diced
240 ml (1 c) cleaned, sliced, fresh morels
60 ml (1/4 c) diced shallots
120 ml (1/2 c) dry red wine
120 ml (1/2 c) white wine
30 ml (2 tbsp) green peppercorns in brine
1 L (4 c) strong beef stock

Put oil in a heavy soup pot on high heat.

When oil begins to smoke add beef and tuna and stir until all sides are dark brown.

While still on high heat, add onion, garlic, morels, shallots and cook and stir for about 2 minutes.

Add the wines and peppercorns and reduce liquid by 1/4.

Add stock and bring to the boil before serving.

Caraway
Serves 6

60 ml (4 tbsp) lard or bacon fat
15 ml (1 tbsp) caraway seeds
60 ml (4 tbsp) flour
1 1/2 L (6 c) water
1 egg, well beaten

Melt the lard or bacon fat in a medium-sized soup pot on low heat.

Add caraway seeds and flour and cook stirring constantly until lightly browned.

Remove from heat, add water and stir until well blended.

Return to heat and cook while stirring until the mixture begins to thicken.

Add **120 ml (1/2 c)** soup to the egg, beat well, and add to the pot – stirring 4 minutes.

Garnish with croutons.

Garlic Croutons

3 slices firm white bread
45 ml (3 tbsp) bacon fat or butter
1 clove garlic, peeled

Trim crusts from bread and cut into **1 cm (1/2 in)** cubes.

Melt butter in small frying pan – add garlic and sauté until lightly brown.

Remove and discard garlic.

Add bread cubes, cook stirring until golden.

Dry on absorbent paper.

Asparagus in Broth
Serves 8

720 ml (3 c) tender asparagus, chopped into **1/2 cm (1/4 in)** pieces after snapping off tough bottoms of stalk.
120 ml (1/2 c) onion, diced
1 large clove garlic, diced
1 thread of saffron
1 1/4 L (5 c) strong chicken stock
30 ml (2 tbsp) shallots, diced

Put all ingredients in your soup pot and bring to a rolling boil.

Boil 4 to 5 minutes.

Poor Man's Stew
Serves 12

60 ml (1/4 c) vegetable oil
680 g (1 1/2 lbs) ground beef
240 ml (1 c) onion, diced
240 ml (1 c) potatoes, diced
15 ml (1 tbsp) minced garlic
120 ml (1/2 c) chili sauce
60 ml (1/4 c) carrots, diced
120 ml (1/2 c) turnip, diced

60 ml (1/4 c) green pepper, diced
1 L (4 c) beef stock
120 ml (1/2 c) cooked rice
240 ml (1 c) frozen peas

Heat oil in a heavy soup pot
on high heat, add beef and cook
on high for 6 to 7 minutes while
stirring until meat is completely
brown.

Add all other ingredients except the
rice and peas and bring to the boil.

Reduce heat and simmer for
20 minutes; add rice and peas.

Return to the boil before serving.

What Did You Do
To My Lobster?
Serves 8

720 ml (3 c) lobster stock*
680 g (1 1/2 lbs) raw lobster meat,
    ground
120 ml (1/2 c) julienne red pepper
120 ml (1/2 c) julienne onion
15 ml (1 tbsp) julienne fresh ginger
45 ml ((3 tbsp) garlic, diced
45 ml (3 tbsp) curry powder
45 ml (3 tbsp) mango chutney
120 ml (1/2 c) Granny Smith apples,
    diced
30 ml (1 oz) "whitewash"
    (equal parts cornstarch and water)

*Readily available as paste or
concentrate in most supermarkets.*

Put all ingredients, except
"whitewash," in your soup pot on
high heat and bring to the boil.

Keep boiling for 4 to 5 minutes.

Whisk in the "whitewash" and boil
until soup begins to thicken.

Chilled Tomato
and Corn
Serves 8

1 1/4 L (5 c) tomato concassée
480 ml (2 c) tomato juice
240 ml (1 c) onion, diced
4 ears of corn (kernels only, please)
120 ml (1/2 c) green pepper,
    diced fine
15 ml (1 tbsp) fresh tarragon,
    chopped
2 bay leaves
15 ml (1 tbsp) garlic, minced

Put all ingredients in a heavy
soup pot and place on medium-
high heat.

Bring slowly to a boil while
stirring.

Reduce heat and simmer
uncovered for 20 minutes –
stirring often.

Remove from the stove and let
stand at room temperature for
60 minutes.

Refrigerate for 6 to 8 hours.

Mix well and serve.

Oyster Mushrooms with Saffron
Serves 8

60 ml (1/4 c) clarified butter
240 ml (1 c) sliced green of the leeks
15 ml (1 tbsp) diced garlic
240 ml (1 c) diced onion
45 ml (3 tbsp) raw, mixed wild rice
13 strands of saffron
1 1/4 L (5 c) sliced, fresh, oyster mushrooms
15 ml (1 tbsp) lemon zest
2 L (8 c) chicken or veal stock
120 ml (1/2 c) grated, 6-year-old white cheddar

Melt butter in a medium-sized soup pot, on high heat.

Add leeks, garlic, onion, and cook on high for 3 to 4 minutes, while stirring.

Add rice and saffron, cooking for 2 more minutes.

Add the mushrooms, zest, and stock and bring to the boil.

Reduce heat and simmer covered for 35 to 40 minutes or until the wild rice begins to open.

Meanwhile, sprinkle equal amounts of cheese into 6 soup bowls.

When soup is ready, pour over the cheese in the soup bowls.

Goat with Red Wine
Serves 10

1 1/2 L (6 c) goat, lamb or beef stock
900 g (2 lbs) boneless goat meat, cut into **1 cm (1/2 in)** cubes and roasted in the oven until golden brown
40 peeled pearl onions
240 ml (1 c) diced double-smoked bacon
2 large cloves of garlic, sliced thin
15 ml (1 tbsp) fresh chopped rosemary
15 ml (1 tbsp) fresh chopped thyme
60 ml (1/4 c) diced green pepper
60 ml (1/4 c) tomato paste
480 ml (2 c) dry red wine
240 ml (1 c) chopped red potatoes, **1 cm (1/2 in)** pieces
120 ml (1/2 c) cooked long grain rice

Pour stock in your soup pot, on high heat, and add the goat meat, onion, bacon, garlic, herbs, green pepper, tomato paste, wine and potatoes and bring to the boil.

Turn heat down to medium-high and simmer covered for 40 minutes.

Then add rice and bring to the boil, on high heat, and serve.

Curried Pork
Serves 8

60 ml (1/4 c) vegetable oil
900 g (2 lbs) diced pork shoulder,
    1 cm (1/2 in) pieces
240 ml (1 c) diced onion
240 ml (1 c) diced green pepper
30 ml (2 tbsp) diced fresh garlic
60 ml (1/4 c) long grain rice
15 ml (1 tbsp) julienne of fresh
    ginger
45 ml (3 tbsp) good curry powder
120 ml (1/2 c) diced red pepper
1 1/2 L (6 c) pork stock
30 ml (2 tbsp) tomato paste
15 ml (1 tbsp) mushroom soy sauce

Pour oil into a medium-sized soup pot and place on high heat, adding pork when oil begins to smoke.

Brown pork on all sides.

Add onion, green pepper, garlic, rice and ginger and cook on high for 5 minutes, while stirring.

Add all other ingredients.

Bring back to the boil, reduce heat and simmer covered for 20 minutes.

Peppered Grouper
Serves 10

115 g (1/4 lb) butter
680 g (1 1/2 lbs) grouper fillets,
    diced 1 cm (1/2 in) pieces
240 ml (1 c) diced onion
240 ml (1 c) diced green pepper
30 ml (2 tbsp) diced garlic
45 ml (3 tbsp) Spanish paprika
45 ml (3 tbsp) green peppercorns
    in brine
15 ml (1 tbsp) dried tarragon
120 ml (1/2 c) chili sauce
60 ml (1/4 c) coarse black pepper
120 ml (1/2 c) good brandy
1 1/2 L (6 c) fish velouté

Put butter and fish into a heavy soup pot on high heat and cook fish for 2 minutes, while stirring gently.

Add onion, green pepper, garlic, paprika, peppercorns, tarragon and chili sauce and cook on high heat for 5 minutes while continuing to stir.

Add coarse black pepper and brandy and cook for 1 minute.

Add velouté.

Reduce heat to medium-high, and bring soup slowly to the boil.

When it has reached a rolling boil, it is ready to serve.

Ham and Yam
Serves 10

480 ml (2 c) shredded yams
680 g (1 1/2 lbs) diced ham,
   1/2 cm (1/4 in) cubes
240 ml (1 c) diced onion
240 ml (1 c) diced leeks
1 clove of garlic, diced
30 ml (2 tbsp) raw long grain rice
1 1/2 L (6 c) ham stock
3 whole cloves
1 cinnamon stick
60 ml (1/4 c) dark brown sugar

Put all ingredients in a medium-sized soup pot and place on high heat.

Bring to a rolling boil, turn heat down and simmer covered for 20 minutes.

Return to high heat and bring back to the boil before serving.

Fall Vegetable with Barley
Serves 12

240 ml (1 c) diced tomatoes
240 ml (1 c) diced onion
240 ml (1 c) diced turnip
120 ml (1/2 c) diced parsnips
120 ml (1/2 c) diced squash

120 ml (1/2 c) diced pumpkin
120 ml (1/2 c) diced leeks
15 ml (1 tbsp) diced garlic
120 ml (1/2 c) chili sauce
1 3/4 L (7 c) vegetable stock
60 ml (4 tbsp) pearl barley,
   uncooked
120 ml (1/2 c) fresh chopped basil

Place all ingredients in a large soup pot, place on high heat and bring to the boil.

Turn heat down and simmer covered for 30 minutes.

Return to the boil before serving.

Chilled Peach with Chocolate
Serves 8

1 1/4 L (5 c) ripe peaches, pitted,
   skinned, and mashed
480 ml (2 c) ricotta cheese
Juice from **2** lemons
720 ml (3 c) 18% cream
240 ml (1 c) shaved white chocolate
480 ml (2 c) French vanilla ice cream
15 ml (1 tbsp) fresh diced mint
60 ml (2 oz) peach brandy

Put all ingredients into a large mixing bowl and whisk together, making sure all of the ice cream has melted.

Cool in the fridge for 2 hours before serving.

Endive Supreme
Serves 14

1 1/4 L (5 c) diced Belgian endive
240 ml (1 c) diced onion
240 ml (1 c) diced leeks
2 strands of saffron
120 ml (1/2 c) sun-dried tomatoes, julienne
15 ml (1 tbsp) diced garlic
30 ml (2 tbsp) dried chanterelle mushrooms
1 1/2 L (6 c) chicken stock
120 ml (1/2 c) 35% cream
2 eggs, beaten
240 ml (1 c) cooked long grain rice
120 ml (1/2 c) shredded St. Agur cheese
Juice from 2 lemons

Place endive, onion, leeks, saffron, tomatoes, garlic and mushrooms along with the stock in your soup pot on high heat.

At the same time put the cream in a small pot on medium heat, and thicken by reducing by half.

Bring soup to a boil and boil for approximately 5 minutes.

Whisk in eggs and add rice.

Whisk in cheese until completely melted.

Add reduced cream, return briefly to the boil, reduce heat and stir in lemon juice.

Oriental Chicken with Watercress
Serves 12

2 L (8 c) chicken stock
30 ml (2 tbsp) Hoisin sauce
30 ml (2 tbsp) light soy sauce
240 ml (1 c) sliced leeks
30 ml (2 tbsp) diced garlic
240 ml (1 c) sliced green pepper
30 ml (2 tbsp) sliced ginger
30 ml (2 tbsp) chopped spearmint
680 g (1 1/2 lbs) chicken, diced
  1 cm (1/2 in) pieces
4 bunches watercress, chopped
  into 3 pieces
120 ml (1/2 c) "whitewash"
  (equal parts cornstarch
  and water)
3 bunches diced green onion

Pour stock, Hoisin sauce and soy sauce in your soup pot; place on high heat, and add leeks, garlic, green pepper, ginger, spearmint, and bring to the boil.

Add chicken to boiling broth.

Add watercress and return to the boil.

Whisk "whitewash" into the boiling soup.

Garnish this soup with green onion and serve.

Garden Vegetable
Serves 10

2 L (8 c) vegetable stock
2 cloves garlic, crushed
480 ml (2 c) diced onion
240 ml (1 c) diced leeks
240 ml (1 c) turnip, cut into
    1 cm (1/2 in) pieces
240 ml (1 c) parsnips, cut into
    1 cm (1/2 in) pieces
240 ml (1 c) carrots, cut into
    1 cm (1/2 in) pieces
240 ml (1 c) sliced mushrooms
240 ml (1 c) chopped broccoli
240 ml (1 c) chopped celery
480 ml (2 c) tomato concassée
60 g (2 oz) dry porcini mushrooms
90 g (3 oz) raw pot barley

Put all ingredients in a large soup pot on high heat.

Bring to the boil, then turn heat down and simmer for 45 minutes.

Curried Ostrich
Serves 12

60 ml (1/4 c) butter
680 g (1 1/2 lbs) boned, cubed
    ostrich meat, 1/2 cm (1/4 in) pieces
240 ml (1 c) Spanish onion, diced
240 ml (1 c) diced red peppers
240 ml (1 c) diced leeks
120 ml (1/2 c) diced celery
120 ml (1/2 c) diced carrots
240 ml (1 c) chopped mango
60 ml (1/4 c) curry powder
3 cloves of garlic, crushed
30 ml (2 tbsp) fresh ginger, julienne
1 3/4 L (7 c) chicken or veal stock
60 ml (1/4 c) long grain rice

Put butter in a heavy soup pot, on high heat.

Add ostrich meat and brown well on all sides.

Add all the other ingredients, still on high heat, and bring to the boil.

Reduce heat and simmer covered for 20 minutes.

Bring back to the boil before serving.

Spicy Beef Stew
Serves 10

680 g (1 1/2 lbs) sirloin steak,
    cut into 1/2 cm (1/4 in) cubes

Brown steak in oven at 200° C (400° F) for 20 minutes.

240 ml (1 c) diced celery
240 ml (1 c) diced onion
240 ml (1 c) diced green pepper
45 ml (3 tbsp) diced garlic
15 ml (1 tbsp) chopped fresh
    oregano
15 ml (1 tbsp) chopped fresh basil

240 ml (1 c) sliced mushrooms
2 L (8 c) tomato concassée
Juice from **2** large lemons
45 ml (3 tbsp) fresh chopped
   coriander

Put all ingredients in a heavy soup pot and place on medium-high heat, stirring occasionally.

Bring to the boil, then reduce heat and simmer covered for 20 minutes.

Note: You may add a bit of powdered beef base to bring out the flavor if desired.

Lamb Ball
Serves 14

Lamb Balls

680 g (1 1/2 lbs) minced lamb
1 egg beaten
5 ml (1 tsp) chopped rosemary
5 ml (1 tsp) chopped thyme
30 ml (2 tbsp) chopped garlic
60 ml (2 oz) chili sauce
30 ml (1 oz) dark soy sauce
60 ml (1/4 c) diced, fried onion
60 ml (1/4 c) plain bread crumbs
5 ml (1 tsp) powdered beef base
5 ml (1 tsp) good seasoning salt

Mix all ingredients thoroughly by hand in a bowl, and roll uniformly sized lamb balls, approximately **2 1/2 cm (1 in)**, the size of a golf ball.

Preheat oven to 190° C (375° F) and bake lamb balls on an oiled baking sheet for approximately 10 minutes.

Soup

60 ml (1/4 c) oil
240 ml (1 c) diced onion
120 ml (1/2 c) diced leeks
3 cloves of garlic, crushed
240 ml (1 c) dried porcini
   mushrooms
240 ml (1 c) diced green pepper
30 ml (2 tbsp) raw long grain rice
120 ml (1/2 c) tomato paste
5 ml (1 tsp) dried rosemary
5 ml (1 tsp) dried thyme
2 1/4 L (9 c) lamb stock
480 ml (2 c) sour cream

Heat oil in a large soup pot on high heat and add onion, leeks, garlic, mushrooms, green pepper and rice and cook for 2 to 3 minutes, still on high heat, while stirring.

Add tomato paste and herbs.

Add stock after one minute, bring to the boil and cook for 15 minutes.

Then add lamb balls and bring to the boil for 2 more minutes before serving

Garnish the top of each bowl with sour cream

Beef Dijon

Serves 10 – 12

60 ml (1/4 c) oil
900 g (2 lbs) sirloin steak, diced
  into **1 cm (1/2 in)** cubes
2 cloves of garlic, minced
240 ml (1 c) diced onions
60 ml (1/4 c) green pepper, diced
15 ml (1 tbsp) green peppercorn
  in brine
120 ml (1/2 c) dry white wine
60 ml (1/4 c) Dijon mustard
1 3/4 L (7 c) beef stock
60 ml (1/4 c) white roux

Heat oil in your soup pot on
high heat.

When the oil is hot, add the beef
and brown well on all sides.

Add garlic, onion, diced pepper,
and peppercorns.

Cook for 2 minutes while stirring.

Add wine and mustard, then add
the stock.

Bring to the boil and keep boiling
for 5 minutes.

Whisk in the roux.

Bring back to the boil before
serving.

Lamb and Orange

Serves 8 – 10

900 g (2 lbs) lamb, diced into
  1 cm (1/2 in) pieces

To brown, bake lamb in the
oven at 200° C (400° F) for 20 to
30 minutes.

240 ml (1 c) sliced green pepper
240 ml (1 c) diced onion
15 ml (1 tbsp) diced garlic
1 240-ml (8-oz) tin frozen
  concentrated orange juice
45 ml (3 tbsp) orange zest
1 L (4 c) lamb stock
1 pinch five-spice powder
4 drops sesame seed oil
60 ml (1/4 c) "whitewash"
  (equal parts cornstarch and water)
30 ml (1 oz) Hoisin sauce

Pre-heat a large wok on high heat.

Add cooked lamb.

Add pepper, onion, garlic, the
frozen orange juice and the zest
and cook on high for 4 to
5 minutes, while stirring.

Add lamb stock, five-spice powder,
and sesame seed oil and bring the
mixture to a boil for approximately
5 minutes.

Whisk in the "whitewash" to
thicken.

Add Hoisin sauce while
whisking well.

Veal Marsala
Serves 10

60 ml (1/4 c) vegetable oil
680 g (1 1/2 lbs) veal, diced into
   1 cm (1/2 in) pieces
480 ml (2 c) shredded chanterelle
   mushrooms
60 ml (1/4 c) diced shallots
15 ml (1 tbsp) diced garlic
240 ml (1 c) Marsala wine
5 ml (1 tsp) chopped fresh thyme
5 ml (1 tsp) green peppercorns
   in brine
2 L (8 c) demi-glace

Pour oil into a heavy soup pot
on high heat.

When oil begins to smoke, add
veal and brown well on all sides,
for 8 to 10 minutes, while stirring.

Add mushrooms, shallots and
garlic and cook on high heat while
stirring for 3 more minutes.

Add Marsala wine, thyme and
peppercorns with brine and bring
to the boil.

Add demi-glace and bring back to
the boil before serving.

Potato and Cucumber
Serves 6

1 medium cucumber
4 medium potatoes, peeled
   and diced
480 ml (2 c) cold water
240 ml (1 c) 35% cream
120 ml (1/2 c) milk
1 green onion, grated
5 ml (1 tsp) dried dill weed or
   15 ml (1 tbsp) chopped fresh dill

Peel the cucumber and slice it
lengthwise. Scoop out seeds with
a spoon, discard seeds and dice
cucumber.

In your soup pot, boil potatoes
in salted water until very soft.

Pour potatoes and liquid into a
sieve, set over a large bowl.

Discard water.

Force potatoes through sieve
or use a food processor.

Return potatoes to your
soup pot.

Stir in cream, milk, grated onion
and the cucumber.

Simmer gently about 5 minutes
or until cucumber is tender.

Add dill and season to taste.

Curried Carrot

Serves 8

480 ml (**2 c**) shredded carrots
120 ml (**1/2 c**) diced onion
120 ml (**1/2 c**) diced green pepper
30 ml (**2 tbsp**) minced garlic
15 ml (**1 tbsp**) julienne of ginger
60 ml (**4 tbsp**) curry powder
120 ml (**1/2 c**) purée of mango
720 ml (**3 c**) vegetable stock
1 1/4 L (**5 c**) béchamel

On high heat, bring carrots, onion, green pepper, garlic, ginger, curry, mango and stock to a boil.

Reduce heat and simmer for 8 to 10 minutes or until it begins to thicken.

Add béchamel.

Bring back to the boil briefly.

Chilled Smoked Chicken Soup with Cranberries

Serves 8 – 10

460 g (**1 lb**) diced smoked chicken,
  1 cm (**1/2 in**) pieces
240 ml (**1 c**) cranberry sauce
240 ml (**1 c**) sour cream
5 ml (**1 tsp**) chopped sage
120 ml (**1/2 c**) dry sherry
Juice from **1** lemon

1 L (**4 c**) 18% cream
240 ml (**8 oz**) fresh orange juice

Put all ingredients in a mixing bowl and whisk together well.

Let stand in the fridge for 8 hours.

Whisk again before serving.

Orange Ruffy Soup with Orange, Lemon and Kiwi

Serves 6

680 g (**1 1/2 lbs**) orange ruffy,
  1 cm (**1/2 in**) cubes
240 ml (**1 c**) fresh orange juice
120 ml (**1/2 c**) lemon juice
240 ml (**1 c**) puréed peeled kiwi
6 strands of saffron
120 ml (**1/2 c**) dry white wine
60 ml (**1/4 c**) diced red pepper
60 ml (**1/4 c**) cooked long grain rice
480 ml (**2 c**) fish stock
4 drops sesame seed oil

Put all ingredients in your soup pot and place on high heat.

Bring to the boil for 3 minutes before serving.

Cream of Lettuce
Serves 8

1 leek, diced
60 ml (1/4 c) butter
120 ml (1/2 c) chopped onion
1 L (4 c) shredded lettuce
60 ml (4 tbsp) flour
15 ml (1 tbsp) chopped parsley
1/2 ml (1/8 tsp) nutmeg
1 1/2 L (6 c) chicken stock
2 egg yolks
120 ml (1/2 c) 35% cream
Shredded lettuce and parsley for
   garnish

Wash leek well, removing all but **5 cm (2 in)** of the green top.

Melt the butter in your soup pot, add chopped onion and leek and sauté until tender.

Add lettuce, cover and simmer for 5 minutes.

Stir in the flour.

Add parsley, seasonings and chicken stock and simmer for 30 minutes.

Purée soup in blender or food processor.

Mix egg yolks and cream in small bowl and stir **60 ml (1/4 c)** hot soup gradually into the mixture.

Add egg mixture to hot soup, stirring constantly.

Heat gently until soup thickens.

Garnish soup with shredded lettuce and parsley.

Note: Use Boston bib or Romaine lettuce for best flavor – not head lettuce.

Chicken in Red Wine
Serves 8

60 ml (1/4 c) vegetable oil
680 g (1 1/2 lbs) raw diced chicken
   – 1/2 cm (1/4 in) pieces
120 ml (1/2 c) diced onion
120 ml (1/2 c) carrots, diced small
45 ml (3 tbsp) diced shallots
240 ml (1 c) dry red wine
15 ml (1 tbsp) chopped sage
1 1/4 L (5 c) demi-glace

Heat oil on high heat in a medium-sized soup pot.

When oil becomes hot, add chicken, onion, carrots and shallots.

Cook for 5 minutes while stirring.

Add wine and sage and cook to reduce by 1/3.

Add demi-glace, bring to the boil and serve.

Ranger Stew
Serves 12

60 ml (1/4 c) vegetable oil
680 g (1 1/2 lbs) diced rabbit meat
   cut into **1 cm (1/2 in)** pieces
230 g (1/2 lb) double-smoked pork
240 ml (1 c) sliced black forest
   mushrooms
120 ml (1/2 c) diced carrots
120 ml (1/2 c) diced turnip
120 ml (1/2 c) diced parsnips
120 ml (1/2 c) diced onion
120 ml (1/2 c) sauerkraut
240 ml (1 c) shredded cabbage
15 ml (1 tbsp) diced garlic
120 ml (1/2 c) chili sauce
60 ml (1/4 c) wild rice
15 ml (1 tbsp) chopped rosemary
2 1/2 L (10 c) game or beef stock
120 ml (1/2 c) Port wine

Heat oil on high heat in a heavy soup pot.

When oil just begins to smoke add rabbit and pork and cook for 8 to 10 minutes.

Then add all the vegetables, garlic, chili sauce, rice and rosemary and cook another 5 minutes.

Then add beef stock and Port.

Bring to the boil.

Reduce heat almost immediately and simmer for 30 minutes.

Swedish Meatball
Serves 10

Meatballs

230 g (1/2 lb) medium ground beef
230 g (1/2 lb) medium ground pork
30 ml (2 tbsp) diced onion
5 ml (1 tsp) diced garlic
1 egg
5 ml (1 tsp) chopped parsley
30 ml (2 tbsp) fine bread crumbs
5 ml (1 tsp) powdered beef base

Put all ingredients in a mixing bowl and mix well by hand.

Pre-heat oven to 190° C (375° F), spray or oil a large baking sheet.

Shape **2 1/2 cm (1 in)** meatballs and bake at 200° C (400° F) for 10 minutes, then take out and cool.

Soup

60 ml (1/4 c) vegetable oil
240 ml (1 c) diced onion
240 ml (1 c) sliced mushrooms
5 ml (1 tsp) diced garlic
240 ml (1 c) beef stock
5 ml (1 tsp) dried tarragon
1 bay leaf
1 3/4 L (7 c) demi-glace
240 ml (1 c) sour cream

Heat oil in your soup pot on high heat.

When oil gets hot, add onion, mushrooms and garlic and cook while stirring on high heat until garlic turns brown.

Add the stock, tarragon and bay leaf and bring to the boil.

Add meatballs and demi-glace and bring to the boil again.

Add sour cream by stirring in gently so as not to break the meatballs.

Canadian Moose
Serves 10 – 12

120 ml (1/2 c) olive oil
900 g (2 lbs) moose meat, diced into 1 cm (1/2 in) cubes
240 ml (1 c) double-smoked pork cut into 1/2 cm (1/4 in) cubes
240 ml (1 c) diced onion
240 ml (1 c) diced green pepper
240 ml (1 c) diced celery
120 ml (1/2 c) diced leek
30 ml (2 tbsp) diced garlic
120 ml (1/2 c) red Port wine
240 ml (1 c) beef stock
2 1/4 L (9 c) seeded, peeled, chopped tomatoes
30 ml (2 tbsp) chopped rosemary
Juice from 2 lemons

Put oil in a heavy soup pot on high heat.

When oil just begins to smoke, add moose meat and cook until meat is dark brown on all sides.

Add pork, onion, pepper, celery, leek and garlic and cook another 5 minutes while stirring.

Add Port and stock and reduce by half.

Add tomatoes and rosemary and bring back to the boil.

Reduce heat, cover, and simmer for 50 minutes.

Add the lemon juice, turn back to high and bring back to the boil before serving.

Chilled Pineapple and Ham
Serves 6

1 pineapple, peeled and puréed
240 ml (1 c) ricotta cheese
120 ml (1/2 c) sour cream
240 ml (1 c) cooked ham, finely diced
720 ml (3 c) 18% cream
30 ml (2 tbsp) white sugar
120 ml (1/2 c) white rum
5 ml (1 tsp) fresh chervil, chopped

Whisk all ingredients together in a large bowl.

Let stand in the fridge for 8 to 12 hours.

Whisk before serving.

Marlin
Serves 12

120 ml (1/2 c) butter
900 g (2 lbs) marlin – skinned,
 boned and cut into **1 cm (1/2 in)**
 pieces
120 ml (1/2 c) diced onion
240 ml (1 c) sliced fresh chanterelle
 mushrooms
120 ml (1/2 c) cooked wild rice
45 ml (3 tbsp) diced garlic
5 ml (1 tsp) chopped fresh oregano
5 ml (1 tsp) fresh chopped coriander
3 strands of saffron
120 ml (1/2 c) diced sun-dried
 tomatoes
120 ml (1/2 c) red pepper, roasted,
 peeled, julienne cut
120 ml (1/2 c) cognac
2 L (8 c) fish stock
3 pheasant eggs – slightly beaten
115 g (1/4 lb) shredded St. Agur
 cheese
45 ml (3 tbsp) beluga caviar

Put butter and fish in a heavy
soup pot, on high heat, and cook
for 5 minutes.

Add onion, mushrooms and
cooked wild rice and cook another
2 minutes.

Add the garlic and herbs and
saffron and cook yet another
2 minutes.

Add sun-dried tomatoes, red
peppers and cognac.

Add fish stock and bring to
the boil.

Whisk in eggs and cheese and
bring back to the boil.

Remove pot from the stove,
folding beluga caviar into soup
before serving.

Anchovies in Cream
Serves 6

90 g (3 oz) whole butter
460 g (1 lb) chopped anchovies
240 ml (1 c) diced onion
120 ml (1/2 c) diced leeks
30 ml (2 tbsp) chopped garlic
45 ml (3 tbsp) chopped capers
2 threads saffron
120 ml (1/2 c) cheap brandy
1 L (4 c) chicken or fish velouté
240 ml (1 c) 35% cream

Put butter, anchovies, onion,
leeks, and garlic in your soup pot,
cooking for 5 minutes on high
heat while stirring.

Add capers, saffron and brandy.

Add the velouté, bring to a boil.

Reduce heat to medium-high for
4 to 5 minutes.

Add cream and bring back to a
boil before serving.

Kale and Potato

Serves 8

4 medium potatoes diced into
    1/2 cm (1/4 in) cubes
30 ml (2 tbsp) vegetable oil
2 L (8 c) water
900 g (2 lbs) fresh kale
230 g (1/2 lb) smoked garlic sausage,
    cooked and sliced

Peel and chop potatoes and add to vegetable oil and water.

Cook for 20 to 30 minutes or until tender.

Remove potatoes and reserve the liquid.

Mash potatoes through a sieve and return to potato liquid.

Simmer for 20 minutes.

Wash kale, discarding any tough leaves and cut into thin shreds.

Add to potatoes and cook for 25 minutes.

Add sausage.

Simmer gently for 5 minutes before serving.

Beef Brisket with Corn

Serves 10

6 large cobs of corn
680 g (1 1/2 lbs) beef brisket, diced
    into **1 cm (1/2 in)** pieces
2 L (8 c) beef stock
120 ml (1/2 c) diced carrots
240 ml (1 c) diced onion
5 ml (1 tsp) diced garlic
240 ml (1 c) diced leeks
30 ml (2 tbsp) demerara sugar
2 whole cloves

Remove kernels from the cobs of corn and reserve.

In medium-sized soup pot put the beef and corn cobs, along with the beef stock, place on high heat and bring to the boil.

When mixture comes to a rolling boil, reduce heat to medium and let simmer for 55 to 60 minutes. (You may have to add a cup or two of water.)

With a set of tongs remove the corn cobs, and discard cobs.

Add all other ingredients, plus the kernels of corn and turn back to high heat.

Bring to the boil, then reduce heat to medium and simmer covered for 20 minutes.

Turn back to high, bring to the boil and serve.

Cream of Diced Lamb
Serves 8

60 ml (1/4 c) vegetable oil
460 g (1 lb) diced lamb − cut into
   1/2 cm (1/4 in) pieces
240 ml (1 c) diced onion
240 ml (1 c) diced green pepper
120 ml (1/2 c) diced leek greens
30 ml (2 tbsp) diced garlic
60 ml (1/4 c) diced carrots
30 ml (2 tbsp) fresh chopped
   rosemary
5 ml (1 tsp) fresh chopped thyme
2 L (8 c) lamb or beef stock
60 g (2 oz) tomato paste
60 ml (1/4 c) light roux
60 ml (1/4 c) 35% cream

Pour oil into a medium-sized soup pot and place on high heat.

When oil begins to smoke, add the lamb and brown on all sides (5 to 6 minutes).

Still on high heat, add onion, green pepper, leeks, garlic, carrots, and herbs, cooking 4 to 5 minutes while stirring constantly.

Stir in stock and tomato paste.

Bring to the boil, reduce to medium heat and simmer covered for 20 minutes.

Return to the boil and whisk in roux.

Slowly add the cream.

Return to the boil one last time before serving.

Ham and Cheese
Serves 8

1 1/2 L (6 c) chicken stock
480 ml (2 c) cubed cooked ham,
   1 cm (1/2 in) pieces
240 ml (1 c) diced onion
30 ml (2 tbsp) diced garlic
120 ml (1/2 c) diced red pepper
60 ml (2 oz) white roux
240 ml (1 c) shredded old cheddar
   cheese
120 ml (1/2 c) Parmesan cheese
120 ml (1/2 c) 35% cream

Put stock, ham onion, garlic and pepper in your soup pot.

Bring to a boil and boil for 3 to 4 minutes.

Whisk in roux.

Once thickened, whisk in the cheeses until completely melted.

Add cream.

Bring back to the boil briefly before serving.

Ground Beef and Cabbage
Serves 12

60 ml (1/4 c) vegetable oil
900 g (2 lbs) ground beef
720 ml (3 c) shredded cabbage
240 ml (1 c) diced onion
240 ml (1 c) sauerkraut
120 ml (1/2 c) diced green onion
120 ml (1/2 c) celery
120 ml (1/2 c) diced carrots
30 ml (2 tbsp) diced garlic
2 L (8 c) beef stock
120 ml (1/2 c) cooked long grain rice

Put oil in your soup pot and place on high heat.

When oil becomes hot, add ground beef and brown.

Add all other ingredients.

Bring to the boil and keep boiling for 8 to 10 minutes, covered.

Poached Mushrooms
Serves 10

1 1/4 L (5 c) strong chicken or veal stock
480 ml (2 c) sliced fresh button mushrooms
240 ml (1 c) oyster mushrooms, sliced

240 ml (1 c) fresh chanterelle mushrooms, sliced
120 ml (1/2 c) dried porcini mushrooms
240 ml (1 c) onion, diced
120 ml (1/2 c) leeks, diced
30 ml (2 tbsp) minced garlic
5 ml (1 tsp) fresh chopped sage

Put all ingredients in your soup pot, on high heat.

Bring to a boil and continue boiling covered for 8 to 10 minutes.

Chilled Banana and Peanut Butter
Serves 6

3 ripe, peeled, puréed bananas
240 ml (1 c) peanut butter
1 L (4 c) 18% cream
Juice from 2 lemons
240 ml (1 c) sour cream
60 ml (1/4 c) shredded coconut
5 ml (1 tsp) orange zest
5 ml (1 tsp) lemon zest
120 ml (1/2 c) Malibu liqueur
5 ml (1 tsp) fresh spearmint, not mint

Put all ingredients in a mixing bowl and whisk together well.

Refrigerate for 12 hours, covered.

Remove from fridge.

Whisk well before serving.

Spicy Beef
Serves 6

60 ml (1/4 c) vegetable oil
680 g (1 1/2 lbs) ground beef
240 ml (1 c) onion, diced
240 ml (1 c) red pepper, diced
2 Scotch bonnet peppers (whole)
120 ml (1/2 c) leeks, diced
30 ml (2 tbsp) chopped garlic
5 ml (1 tsp) chili powder
240 ml (1 c) chili sauce
720 ml (3 c) tomato sauce
1 bay leaf

Pour oil in a heavy soup pot on high heat.

When oil is hot add beef, onion, pepper, leeks and garlic.

Still on high heat, stir and cook until onion, leeks and garlic are golden brown.

Add chili powder, chili sauce, tomato sauce and bay leaf.

Bring to the boil.

Reduce heat and simmer uncovered for 5 minutes.

Oysters with Stilton and Saffron
Serves 4

30 ml (2 tbsp) butter
120 ml (1/2 c) shallots, diced fine
120 ml (1/2 c) leeks, diced fine –
    yellow part only
3 strands of saffron
20 fresh shucked oysters
    (reserve the juice)
60 ml (1/4 c) Riesling wine
600 ml (2 1/2 c) 35% cream
120 ml (1/2 c) grated Stilton cheese

Melt butter in a saucepan over medium-high heat.

Add shallots, leeks, saffron and oysters, cooking slowly for 3 to 4 minutes, while stirring.

Add wine and the juice from the oysters, reduce liquid by 1/4.

Add cream and reduce by 10 percent.

Stir in cheese before serving.

Tomato Vegetable with Barley
Serves 12

720 ml (3 c) vegetable stock
40 peeled, seeded and diced plum tomatoes
240 ml (1 c) diced onion
240 ml (1 c) diced carrots
240 ml (1 c) diced celery
240 ml (1 c) diced parsnips
120 ml (1/2 c) diced leeks
60 g (2 oz) sun-dried tomatoes, sliced
45 ml (3 tbsp) pearl barley
120 ml (1/2 c) chopped fresh basil
45 ml (3 tbsp) dried porcini mushrooms

Put all ingredients in a large soup pot on high heat.

Bring to the boil, stirring occasionally.

When soup reaches a rolling boil, reduce heat to medium and simmer covered for 35 to 40 minutes.

Return to the boil before serving.

Trout Chowder
Serves 12

680 g (1 1/2 lbs) skinned, de-boned, diced fresh trout
240 ml (1 c) diced onion
240 ml (1 c) diced celery
240 ml (1 c) diced new potatoes
30 ml (2 tbsp) diced garlic
120 ml (1/2 c) diced cooked ham
120 ml (1/2 c) diced leeks
240 ml (1 c) cleaned fresh fiddleheads
240 ml (1 c) cooked wild rice
1 1/2 L (6 c) fish stock
240 ml (1 c) lager beer
120 ml (1/2 c) aged white cheddar, shredded

Put all ingredients except cheese into your soup pot.

Bring to the boil on high heat.

Reduce heat and simmer for 10 minutes.

Turn back to high and bring to the boil one more time.

Whisk in cheese until completely melted and serve.

Wieners and Beans
Serves 8

2 3/4 L (11 c) dark beef stock
240 ml (1 c) dried white beans
1 L (4 c) sliced wieners,
   1 cm (1/2 in) slices
240 ml (1 c) diced onion
120 ml (1/2 c) diced side bacon
60 ml (1/4 c) mushrooms
1 clove garlic, chopped
3 whole cloves
1/2 stick cinnamon

Pour stock into a large soup pot and add beans, set on high heat and bring to the boil, covered.

Reduce heat and let simmer for 2 hours.

Add the rest of the ingredients.

Bring back to the boil.

Reduce heat and simmer covered for 20 minutes.

Mom's
Beef Stew
Serves 10

900 g (2 lbs) inside round steak, diced in 1 cm (1/2 in) cubes

Put in a 200° C (400° F) oven for 20-30 minutes or until golden brown.

2 3/4 L (11 c) beef stock
240 ml (1 c) diced onion
240 ml (1 c) diced carrots
240 ml (1 c) diced turnip
240 ml (1 c) diced potatoes
30 ml (2 tbsp) chopped garlic
240 ml (1 c) diced celery
120 ml (1/2 c) diced green pepper
120 ml (1/2 c) tomato paste
60 ml (1/4 c) raw pearl barley
60 ml (1/4 c) chopped fresh basil

Put all ingredients, including beef, into a large soup pot on high heat and bring to the boil.

Reduce heat and simmer covered for 60 minutes.

Beef Noodle
with Sirloin
Serves 12

900 g (2 lbs) sirloin steak, cut into 1/2 cm (1/4 in) pieces

Place on a baking sheet and bake at 200° C (400° F) until golden brown.

240 ml (1 c) Spanish onion, diced
240 ml (1 c) celery, diced
240 ml (1 c) carrots, diced
240 ml (1 c) turnip diced
120 ml (1/2 c) green pepper, diced
2 cloves of garlic, diced
120 ml (1/2 c) parsnips, diced
240 ml (1 c) tomato paste

2 L (8 c) beef stock
5 ml (1 tsp) dried tarragon
480 ml (2 c) medium egg noodles
(pre-cooked to al dente)

Put all ingredients except noodles in your soup pot, place on high heat, and bring to the boil.

Reduce heat and simmer, covered, for 40 minutes.

Add noodles, return back to the boil until noodles are perfectly tender.

Saffron and Mussels
Serves 6 – 8

60 ml (1/4 c) whole butter
240 ml (1 c) diced leeks
240 ml (1 c) Spanish onion, diced
5 ml (1 tsp) minced fresh garlic
12 strands of saffron
240 ml (1 c) dry white wine
1 1/4 L (5 c) chicken or fish stock
900 g (2 lbs) scrubbed, cultured
mussels

Melt butter in a medium soup pot on high heat.

Add leeks, onion, and garlic and cook on high heat, while stirring, for 3 to 6 minutes.

Then add saffron and wine and reduce by half.

Still on high heat, add stock and bring to the boil.

Still on high heat, add mussels in shells.

Continue cooking for 8 to 10 minutes until mussels have opened.

An equal count of mussels in each bowl, please.

Cream of Fresh Tomato
Serves 12

40 peeled, seeded, and chopped
plum tomatoes
120 ml (1/2 c) extra virgin olive oil
240 ml (1 c) fine diced onion
120 ml (1/2 c) fine diced green
pepper
5 ml (1 tsp) diced garlic
240 ml (1 c) 35% cream

Place chopped tomatoes in a heavy soup pot, on medium-high heat, and cook stirring occasionally for 45 to 50 minutes.

Remove tomatoes from purée.

Rinse pot, add oil and place back on high heat.

Add onion, green pepper and garlic, cooking on high heat while stirring for 5 to 6 minutes.

Add the tomato purée to the pot containing the onion, garlic and green pepper.

Bring to the boil while stirring in cream. Serve.

Royal Chicken
Serves 10

60 ml (1/4 c) clarified butter
900 g (2 lbs) diced raw chicken,
cut into **1/2 cm (1/4 in)** pieces
120 ml (1/2 c) diced onion
120 ml (1/2 c) diced leeks
15 ml (1 tbsp) diced garlic
60 ml (1/4 c) fine diced red pepper
5 ml (1 tsp) chopped fresh tarragon
120 ml (1/2 c) dry white wine
1 1/2 L (6 c) chicken stock
60 ml (1/4 c) buerre-manié
60 ml (1/4 c) 35% cream

Put butter in a medium-sized soup pot on high heat.

Add chicken and cook for 5 minutes, while stirring.

Then add onion, leeks, garlic, red pepper, and tarragon, while still on high heat, and cook for another 5 minutes, still stirring.

Then deglaze the pan by adding the wine, stir up well and add to the pot.

Add stock, still on high heat, and bring to the boil.

Add small amounts of the boiling stock to the beurre-manié, whisking until it becomes a smooth paste.

Whisk beurre-manié and cream into the soup.

Bring to the boil and serve.

Smoked Chicken Gazpacho
Serves 8 – 10

1 1/2 L (6 c) tomato juice
240 ml (1 c) diced onion
460 g (1 lb) double-smoked
chicken, **1/2 cm (1/4 in)** cubes
240 ml (1 c) diced carrots
240 ml (1 c) diced celery
480 ml (2 c) diced green pepper
30 ml (2 tbsp) diced garlic
5 ml (1 tsp) chopped fresh oregano
1 small jalapeno pepper diced
3 plum tomatoes, peeled, seeded, chopped
30 ml (2 tbsp) white sugar
80 ml (1/3 c) red wine vinegar
Juice from **1** lemon
30 ml (2 tbsp) fresh chopped coriander

Put all ingredients in a heavy soup pot.

Place on medium-high heat and bring to a boil slowly.

When the soup reaches the boil, turn heat down and simmer covered for 35 to 40 minutes.

Note: You must stir constantly throughout the entire cooking time.

Place in the fridge for 8 to 10 hours, stir and serve.

Smoked Duck
with
Watercress
Serves 10

1 1/2 L (6 c) duck or chicken stock
360 ml (1 1/2 c) smoked duck,
    diced in **1 cm (1/2 in)** cubes
240 ml (1 c) diced onion
30 ml (2 tbsp) diced roasted red
    pepper
1 anise star
1 clove garlic, minced
3 bunches of watercress, each
    chopped into **3** equal portions
60 ml (1/4 c) white roux
30 ml (1 oz) Hoisin sauce

Pour stock in a medium-sized pot, on high heat.

Then add duck, onion, red pepper, anise star and garlic.

Return to the boil, then add chopped watercress.

Return again to the boil and whisk in roux.

Return to the boil one last time and add Hoisin sauce before serving.

Bacon and Beef
with
Porcini Mushrooms
Serves 12

60 ml (1/4 c) olive oil
680 g (1 1/2 lbs) diced round steak,
    1 cm (1/2 in) pieces
230 g (1/2 lbs) diced side bacon,
    1 cm (1/2 in) pieces
240 ml (1 c) diced onions
120 ml (1/2 c) diced green pepper
5 ml (1 tsp) diced garlic
120 ml (1/2 c) dry red wine
5 ml (1 tsp) dried tarragon
2 bay leaves
60 ml (1/4 c) tomato paste
115 g (4 oz) dried porcini mushrooms
2 L (8 c) demi-glace

Pour oil into a heavy soup pot, on high heat.

When oil just begins to smoke, add beef and cook until meat is browned on all sides.

Add bacon and cook for 4 minutes while stirring.

Add onion, green pepper, garlic and cook for another 2 minutes while stirring.

Add wine, tarragon, bay leaves, tomato paste and mushrooms and bring to the boil.

Add demi-glace.

Return to the boil before serving.

Morel and Tomato
Serves 10

120 ml (1/2 c) extra virgin olive oil
12 fresh morel mushrooms, cleaned and sliced
3 cloves garlic, diced
240 ml (1 c) diced onion
120 ml (1/2 c) diced green pepper
6 fennel seeds
2 bay leaves
5 ml (1 tsp) chopped fresh oregano
240 ml (1 c) dry red wine
1 1/2 L (6 c) tomato concassée

Pour oil in a heavy soup pot on high heat.

When oil becomes hot add mushrooms, garlic, onion, pepper, fennel, bay leaves and oregano and cook on high heat while stirring, until the garlic turns golden brown.

Add the wine and bring back to the boil.

Add tomato concassée.

Reduce heat to medium and cook for 35 to 40 minutes, stirring occasionally.

Decadent Chilled Lobster
Serves 8

460 g (1 lbs) ground lobster meat
240 ml (1 c) sour cream
480 ml (2 c) chili sauce
45 ml (3 tbsp) horseradish
5 ml (1 tsp) fresh chopped tarragon
120 ml (1/2 c) lemon juice
3 strands of saffron
240 ml (1 c) lobster stock, or
    5 ml (1 tsp) lobster base in
    240 ml (1 c) water
5 ml (1 tsp) diced garlic
30 ml (2 tbsp) beluga caviar
720 ml (3 c) 18% cream

Put all ingredients in a mixing bowl and whisk together well.

Let stand in fridge for 8 to 10 hours.

Whisk well before serving.

Smoked Turkey with Beans
Serves 12

2 1/2 L (10 c) chicken stock
900 g (2 lbs) double-smoked turkey, diced into 1 cm (1/2 in) pieces
120 ml (1/2 c) white navy beans
240 ml (1 c) diced onion
120 ml (1/2 c) diced leeks

2 cloves garlic, diced
120 ml (1/2 c) diced celery
60 ml (1/4 c) diced carrots
120 ml (1/2 c) diced green pepper
30 ml (2 tbsp) fresh chopped
    rosemary
2 bay leaves

Put all ingredients in your soup pot on high heat and bring to the boil.

Reduce heat and simmer covered for 1 1/2 hours.

Note: Check the beans to see if they are cooked to your liking. (If not, simmer on medium heat for another 20 minutes.)

Corned Beef and Cabbage
Serves 10

1 1/2 L (6 c) corned beef broth
900 g (2 lbs) cooked corned beef
    cut into **1 cm (1/2 in)** cubes
    (leftover corned beef is fine)
240 ml (1 c) diced onion
720 ml (3 c) shredded cabbage
5 ml (1 tsp) diced garlic
60 ml (1/4 c) diced carrots
60 ml (1/4 c) sauerkraut
60 ml (1/4 c) diced potatoes

Put all ingredients in your soup pot on high heat and bring to the boil.

Reduce heat and simmer for 20 minutes before serving.

Braised Beef with Pearl Onions
Serves 8

60 ml (1/4 c) vegetable oil
680 g (1 1/2 lbs) diced flank steak,
    cut into **1 cm (1/2 in)** pieces
1 1/2 L (6 c) peeled pearl onions
5 ml (1 tsp) diced garlic
240 ml (1 c) diced green pepper
240 ml (1 c) sliced oyster mushrooms
120 ml (1/2 c) tomato paste
1 1/2 L (6 c) strong beef stock
120 ml (1/2 c) "whitewash"
    (equal parts cornstarch and water)
60 ml (2 oz) Hoisin sauce

Pour oil into a medium-sized soup pot and place on high heat.

When oil just begins to smoke add beef and brown on all sides, about 5 to 6 minutes.

Add onion, garlic, green pepper and mushrooms, still on high heat, stir for 4 to 5 minutes, then stir in tomato paste.

Add stock while still on high heat and bring to a boil.

When soup reaches a rolling boil, whisk in "whitewash," add Hoisin sauce and serve.

Smoked Ham Florentine

Serves 10

680 g (1 1/2 lbs) chopped smoked ham, **1/2 cm (1/4 in)** pieces
120 ml (1/2 c) diced onion
1 clove of garlic minced
30 ml (2 tbsp) chopped rosemary
120 ml (1/2 c) white wine
2 L (8 c) ham stock
900 g (2 lbs) spinach, cleaned and chopped
60 ml (1/4 c) cooked long grain rice
2 eggs, beaten
120 ml (1/2 c) grated Tuscanello cheese

Place ham, wine, onion, minced garlic, rosemary and stock in a pot on high heat and bring to the boil.

Add spinach and rice and leave on high.

Mix eggs and cheese together in a bowl.

When soup returns to the boil, whisk in egg and cheese mixture and whisk for 2 minutes.

Remove from heat and serve.

Red Snapper

Serves 10

60 ml (1/4 c) butter
900 g (2 lbs) cleaned filleted red snapper, diced in **1 cm (1/2 in)** pieces
120 ml (1/2 c) sliced onion
120 ml (1/2 c) sliced green pepper
60 ml (1/4 c) sliced red pepper
1 jalapeno pepper chopped
60 ml (1/4 c) diced garlic
30 ml (2 tbsp) Spanish paprika
120 ml (1/2 c) chili sauce
1 anise star
5 ml (1 tsp) dried oregano
720 ml (3 c) tomato sauce
480 ml (2 c) fish stock
60 ml (4 tbsp) chopped fresh coriander
120 ml (1/2 c) cooked long grain rice

Place heavy soup pot on high heat, add butter, fish, onion, green and red pepper, jalapeno pepper and garlic.

Cook, while stirring, until the garlic turns golden brown.

Add paprika, chili sauce, anise star, oregano, tomato sauce, fish stock and coriander.

Bring the soup to the boil.

Add rice and stir before serving.

Green Pea Soup with Mint
Serves 6

720 ml (3 c) shelled fresh peas
1 1/4 L (5 c) chicken stock
160 ml (1/4 c) 35% cream
30 ml (2 tbsp) finely chopped mint

Cook the peas until tender in very lightly salted water, drain and purée them in a blender.

Add the chicken stock and cream and blend until smooth.

Reheat and just before serving stir in the mint.

Chilled Shrimp with Lime
Serves 8

480 ml (2 c) cooked cocktail shrimps
240 ml (1 c) lime sherbet, frozen
120 ml (1/2 c) lime juice
480 ml (2 c) sour cream
5 ml (1 tsp) chopped dill weed
30 ml (2 tbsp) zest of lime, from
   a zester
1 L (4 c) 18% cream
5 ml (1 tsp) beluga caviar

Put all ingredients in a mixing bowl and whisk until smooth but leaving the shrimp whole.

Then let stand in the fridge, covered, for 8 hours.

Whisk lightly and serve.

Ham and Sour Cream
Serves 12

2 L (8 c) ham or chicken stock
900 g (2 lbs) smoked ham diced
   into **1 cm (1/2 in)** cubes
480 ml (2 c) sauerkraut
240 ml (1 c) diced onion
30 ml (2 tbsp) diced parsley
60 ml (1/4 c) diced carrots
60 ml (1/4 c) diced green pepper
240 ml (1 c) shredded cabbage
2 juniper berries
2 bay leaves
45 ml (3 tbsp) caraway seeds
240 ml (1 c) sour cream

Put all ingredients except sour cream in your soup pot on high heat and bring to the boil.

Reduce heat and simmer for 20 minutes.

Stir in sour cream before serving.

Remove from heat and serve.

Calabria with Olives
Serves 12

120 ml (1/2 c) extra virgin olive oil
240 ml (1 c) diced onion
30 ml (2 tbsp) diced garlic
240 ml (1 c) diced green pepper
240 ml (1 c) diced leeks
120 ml (1/2 c) diced fennel
680 g (1 1/2 lbs) Calabria salami
   (Have your butcher grind it.)
240 ml (1 c) sliced good green olives
1 1/2 L (6 c) tomato concassée
5 ml (1 tsp) chopped fresh oregano
480 ml (2 c) tomato juice

Pour oil in a large soup pot on high heat, when oil gets hot add onion, garlic, green pepper, leeks and fennel.

Cook on high heat until brown, then add salami, olives, tomatoes, oregano and the tomato juice.

Bring to the boil, then turn heat down and simmer for 20 minutes.

Bring back to the boil and serve.

Cream of Coriander
Serves 10

240 ml (1 c) diced onion
240 ml (1 c) diced leeks
240 ml (1 c) roasted red peppers, chopped

3 bunches coriander, chopped
8 cloves of roasted garlic, chopped
1 Scotch bonnet pepper, diced
1 3/4 L (7 c) chicken stock
120 ml (1/2 c) cooked long grain rice
90 ml (6 tbsp) white roux
120 ml (1/2 c) 35% cream*

Put all ingredients, except the roux and cream in a medium-sized soup pot and place on high heat.

Bring to the boil and cook for 5 minutes.

While still boiling, mix in the roux.

Bring back to the boil and serve.

*Note: 120 ml (1/2 c) cream is optional and should be stirred into soup before serving.

Atlantic Sole
Serves 10

60 ml (1/4 c) butter
680 g (1 1/2 lbs) Atlantic sole fillets, cut into 1/2 cm (1/4 in) pieces
240 ml (1 c) diced onion
240 ml (1 c) diced leeks
5 ml (1 tsp) diced garlic
240 ml (1 c) tomato concassée
5 ml (1 tsp) chopped tarragon
240 ml (1 c) dry white wine
30 ml (1 oz) lemon juice
5 ml (1 tsp) lemon zest, from a zester
1 1/2 L (6 c) fish velouté
480 ml (2 c) shredded Asiago cheese

In a heavy soup pot, melt butter on high heat.

When the butter has melted add sole, onion, leeks, garlic and cook for 5 minutes, while stirring.

Add tomatoes and tarragon and cook for 5 minutes more.

Add wine and reduce by 1/3.

Add lemon juice, zest and the velouté and bring to the boil.

Whisk in the Asiago cheese until it is completely melted.

Remove from stove and serve.

Shark with Demi-Glace
Serves 12

60 ml (1/4 c) butter
900 g (2 lbs) Mako shark – boned, skinned and diced, **1 cm (1/2 in)** pieces
120 ml (1/2 c) peeled, chopped shallots
120 ml (1/2 c) Madeira wine
480 ml (2 c) shark or fish stock
90 g (3 oz) dried bolete mushrooms
30 g (1 oz) tomato paste
1 1/2 L (6 c) demi-glace

Put butter and fish in a heavy soup pot on high heat and cook for 4 minutes, while stirring.

Then add shallots and cook until brown.

Then add Madeira and reduce by half.

Add stock and mushrooms and reduce again by half.

Add tomato paste and demi-glace.

Bring back to the boil and serve.

Potato, Bacon and Cheese
Serves 10

1 L (4 c) diced potatoes, **1/2 cm (1/4 in)** pieces
230 g (1/2 lb) cooked chopped bacon
240 ml (1 c) diced onion
5 ml (1 tsp) chopped garlic
60 ml (1/4 c) diced leeks
30 ml (2 tbsp) diced red pepper
2 L (8 c) chicken stock
60 ml (2 oz) white roux
240 ml (1 c) shredded medium cheddar cheese
120 ml (1/2 c) grated Parmesan cheese

Reserve the roux and cheese.

Put all other ingredients in your soup pot, on high heat, and bring to the boil.

Reduce heat and simmer for 20 minutes.

Return to the boil and whisk in roux.

Finally, whisk in cheeses until completely melted.

Chilled Pear with Lemon Saffron

Serves 10

1 L (4 c) peeled, seeded and puréed pear pulp
240 ml (1 c) sour cream
120 ml (1/2 c) ricotta cheese
60 ml (1/4 c) lemon juice
30 ml (2 tbsp) zest of orange from a zester
4 threads of saffron
60 ml (2 oz) Marsala wine
1 L (4 c) 18% cream
120 ml (4 oz) lemon marmalade

Put all ingredients in a mixing bowl and whisk together well.

Let stand in the fridge for 8 hours.

Whisk again before serving.

Lobster

Serves 12

680 g (1 1/2 lbs) lobster meat, cut into 1 cm (1/2 in) pieces
15 little neck clams
15 mussels
25 shrimp
240 ml (1 c) diced onion
2 cloves of garlic, diced
240 ml (1 c) diced leeks
120 ml (1/2 c) chili sauce
240 ml (1 c) sliced oyster mushrooms

3 strands of saffron
2 3/4 L (11 c) lobster or fish stock
120 ml (1/2 c) brandy
240 ml (1 c) shredded white 6-year-old cheddar

Put all ingredients, except brandy, and cheese in a large soup pot on high heat and bring to a boil.

Reduce heat to medium-high and simmer covered for 15 minutes, or until the clams open.

Stir in brandy and cheese.

Remove from stove and serve.

Mango Chicken

Serves 10

60 ml (1/4 c) butter
680 g (1 1/2 lbs) raw chicken meat, diced into 1 cm (1/2 in) pieces
1 Scotch bonnet pepper, chopped
240 ml (1 c) diced red pepper
240 ml (1 c) diced scallions
720 ml (3 c) peeled, pitted mango, puréed
120 ml (1/2 c) coconut milk
30 ml (2 tbsp) chopped coriander
720 ml (3 c) chicken stock
240 ml (1 c) sour cream
Juice from 1 lemon
120 ml (1/2 c) cooked black-eyed peas

Melt butter in your soup pot, on high heat.

Add chicken, peppers and scallions and cook on high heat for 5 minutes while stirring.

Add mango, coconut milk, coriander, chicken stock and bring to the boil.

Add sour cream, lemon juice and peas and bring back to the boil.

Old Fashioned Beef Noodle
Serves 14

60 ml (1/4 c) oil
900 g (2 lbs) round steak,
    diced into **1 cm (1/2 in)** pieces
240 ml (1 c) diced onion
240 ml (1 c) peeled pearl onions
240 ml (1 c) diced leeks
240 ml (1 c) diced carrot
240 ml (1 c) diced celery
120 ml (1/2 c) sliced mushrooms
2 1/2 L (12 c) beef stock
5 ml (1 tsp) dried tarragon
120 ml (1/2 c) tomato paste
115 g (4 oz) dry, medium-broad
    egg noodles

Heat oil in a heavy soup pot on high heat.

When oil just begins to smoke, add beef and cook until dark brown on all sides.

Add all other ingredients, except noodles, and bring to the boil.

Reduce heat and simmer for 20 minutes.

Turn heat back to high, bring soup to the boil, and add noodles.

Cook for 5 minutes.

Genoa Salami
Serves 12

60 ml (1/4 c) extra virgin olive oil
240 ml (1 c) diced leeks
240 ml (1 c) diced onion
240 ml (1 c) diced green pepper
240 ml (1 c) diced fennel
30 ml (2 tbsp) diced fresh garlic
2 L (8 c) tomato concassée
60 ml (1/4 c) diced green olives
460 g (1 lb) Genoa salami
    (ground by your butcher)
480 ml (2 c) chicken stock
60 ml (1/4 c) tomato paste

Pour oil into a medium-sized soup pot and place on high heat.

Add leeks, onion, green pepper, fennel and garlic and cook on high heat for 5 to 6 minutes while stirring.

Add concassée and bring to the boil, reduce to medium heat and simmer for 20 minutes.

Add the rest of the ingredients.

Return to the boil before serving.

Lamb Fusilli
Serves 10

900 g (2 lbs) cooked lamb,
  cut into **1 cm (1/2 in)** pieces
3 cloves garlic, diced
60 ml (2 oz) Port wine
240 ml (1 c) diced onion
120 ml (1/2 c) finely diced green
  pepper
120 ml (1/2 c) diced carrots
120 ml (1/2 c) tomato paste
30 ml (2 tbsp) fresh rosemary,
  chopped
2 bay leaves
1 1/2 L (6 c) beef stock
240 ml (1 c) fusilli pasta, uncooked

Put the lamb on a baking sheet, salt and pepper the meat and sprinkle the garlic over the meat.

Place in a pre-heated oven, 200° C (400° F), and bake for 40 to 50 minutes.

When done, remove from oven, deglaze the pan with the Port; put the meat and the renderings into your soup pot with all other ingredients, except the fusilli.

Place the pot on high heat, bring to the boil.

Reduce heat and simmer covered for 30 to 40 minutes.

Return to the boil, add fusilli and boil for 12 more minutes before serving.

Chicken Pesto
Serves 10

60 ml (1/4 c) olive oil
680 g (1 1/2 lbs) raw chicken,
  cut into **1 cm (1/2 in)** pieces
120 ml (1/2 c) diced onion
240 ml (1 c) diced leeks
5 ml (1 tsp) chopped garlic
240 ml (1 c) chicken stock
240 ml (1 c) chopped fresh basil
1 1/2 L (6 c) chicken velouté
120 ml (1/2 c) roasted pine nuts
60 ml (1/4 c) 35% cream

Heat oil in your soup pot on high heat.

Add chicken, onion and leeks and cook while stirring, approximately 6 minutes.

Add garlic and cook another 2 minutes, or until garlic is golden brown.

Add stock and basil and cook another 2 minutes.

Add velouté and bring back to the boil.

Add nuts and cream.

Return to the boil before serving.

Shepherd's Pie
Serves 8

60 ml (1/4 c) oil
680 g (1 1/2 lbs) ground lamb
120 ml (1/2 c) diced onion
120 ml (1/2 c) diced green pepper
120 ml (1/2 c) finely diced carrots
5 ml (1 tsp) chopped garlic
2 ml (1/2 tsp) diced thyme
5 ml (1 tsp) tomato paste
120 ml (1/2 c) frozen peas
1 L (4 c) lamb stock
240 ml (1 c) mashed potatoes

Put oil in soup pot, on high heat.

Add lamb and cook for 6 to 8 minutes, while stirring.

Add onion, green pepper, carrots, garlic, thyme and cook for another 5 minutes.

Add tomato paste, peas and stock, and bring to a boil; turn heat down and simmer for 20 minutes.

Put in a casserole dish and spread mashed potatoes over top.

Heat in a 200° C (400° F) oven until brown.

Spaghetti
Serves 10

120 ml (1/2 c) virgin olive oil
240 ml (1 c) diced onion
240 ml (1 c) diced green pepper
3 cloves of garlic, chopped
480 ml (2 c) fresh fennel, chopped
240 ml (1 c) sliced mushrooms
5 ml (1 tsp) chili peppers
2 L (8 c) tomato concassée
2 bay leaves
5 ml (1 tsp) dried oregano
720 ml (3 c) spaghetti cooked al dente and snipped with scissors into **2 1/2 cm (1 in)** pieces

Pour oil into a heavy soup pot on high heat.

Add onion, green pepper, garlic, fennel, mushrooms and chili pepper, and cook on high heat until the garlic turns brown.

Add concassée, bay leaves, and oregano and bring to the boil.

Reduce heat and simmer for 30 minutes, while stirring occasionally.

Bring back to the boil, add spaghetti and serve.

Liza's Classic Lobster

Serves 10

60 g (2 oz) whole sweet butter
680 g (1 1/2 lbs) raw lobster meat diced **1 cm (1/2 in)**
240 ml (1 c) diced onions
5 ml (1 tsp) diced garlic
115 g (4 oz) sun-dried tomato
30 ml (2 tbsp) Spanish paprika
30 ml (2 tbsp) fresh oregano
1 L (4 c) sliced strawberries
60 ml (2 oz) champagne
90 ml (3 oz) Pernod
1 3/4 L (7 c) lobster stock
60 g (2 oz) goat cheese

Add butter to hot soup pot.

As butter begins to brown, add lobster, onions, garlic, sun-dried tomato, paprika, oregano and strawberries and cook on high heat for 5 to 6 minutes, stirring frequently.

Add champagne, Pernod, and flambé.

Add lobster stock after warming in a separate pot.

Add goat cheese and melt completely while stirring.

Bring to boil and serve.

Shrimp Soprano

Serves 12

120 ml (1/2 c) extra virgin olive oil
900 g (2 lbs) cleaned, peeled shrimp (30–35)
120 ml (1/2 c) diced onion
120 ml (1/2 c) diced green pepper
60 ml (1/4 c) chopped garlic
60 ml (1/4 c) diced fennel
120 ml (1/2 c) sliced mushrooms
30 ml (2 tbsp) chopped fresh oregano
480 ml (2 c) fish stock
1 1/2 L (6 c) tomato sauce
120 ml (1/2 c) grated Tuscanello cheese

Heat oil in your soup pot on high heat.

When oil is hot add shrimp, onion, pepper, garlic, fennel, and mushrooms and cook for 5 minutes, still on high heat, while stirring.

Add oregano and cook for 1 more minute.

Then add the stock, bring back to the boil and reduce by 1/4.

Add tomato sauce and bring soup back to the boil.

Whisk in the cheese and keep whisking until cheese is completely melted. Serve.

Lamb Goulash

Serves 8 – 10

120 ml (1/2 c) olive oil
230 g (1/2 lb) minced lamb
120 ml (1/2 c) diced onions
120 ml (1/2 c) diced carrots
120 ml (1/2 c) diced green peppers
120 ml (1/2 c) sliced sun-dried
    tomatoes
240 ml (1 c) finely diced yams
30 ml (2 tbsp) diced garlic
120 ml (1/2 c) tomato paste
30 ml (2 tbsp) fresh rosemary
5 ml (1 tsp) diced fresh thyme
120 ml (4 oz) chili sauce
1 1/4 L (5 c) lamb or beef stock
60 ml (2 oz) sour cream

Put oil in medium-sized soup pot on high heat.

When oil gets hot, add lamb and cook until browned well, stirring occasionally.

Add all other ingredients except the sour cream and bring to a boil.

Turn heat down and simmer uncovered for 20 minutes.

Return to a boil.

Whisk in the sour cream and serve.

Peachy Shrimp

Serves 4 – 6

120 ml (1/2 c) whole butter
230 g (1/2 lb) diced raw shrimp
120 ml (1/2 c) finely diced leek
120 ml (1/2 c) diced onions
5 ml (1 tsp) diced shallots
4 peaches, peeled, pitted and
    quartered
30 ml (2 tbsp) demerara sugar
8 ml (1/2 tbsp) fresh chopped
    tarragon
1 L (4 c) shrimp stock made from
    shrimp shells
240 ml (1 c) bourbon

Heat butter on high in medium-sized soup pot.

When butter begins to bubble, add shrimp, leeks, onions, shallots and peaches.

Still on high, stir constantly for 6 to 8 minutes.

Add sugar and tarragon.

Cook together for 30 to 60 seconds.

Add shrimp stock and bourbon.

Bring to a boil and serve.

Vegetable Soup with Chervil

Serves 8

240 ml (1 c) carrots, cut in thick slices
1 1/4 L (5 c) chicken stock
240 ml (1 c) turnip, cut in chunks
60 ml (1/4 c) zucchini, cut into thick slices
60 ml (1/4 c) 35% cream
30 ml (2 tbsp) chopped chervil

Bring sliced carrots and chicken stock to a boil, on high heat; lower heat and simmer for 5 minutes.

Add turnip and cook for another 10 minutes.

Add the zucchini and cook for 12 to 15 minutes more until all vegetables are tender.

Put through a coarse food mill or purée briefly in a blender.

Reheat before serving, stir in cream and chopped chervil.

Mutton Ragout

Serves 8 – 10

900 g (2 lbs) mutton cut into 1 cm (1/2 in) cubes
240 ml (1 c) diced onions
120 ml (1/2 c) diced green peppers
240 ml (1 c) diced carrots
120 ml (1/2 c) diced turnip
120 ml (1/2 c) diced leek
360 ml (1 1/2 c) diced potato in 1 cm (1/2 in) cubes
60 g (2 oz) tomato paste
2 1/2 L (10 c) beef stock
60 g (2 oz) pearl barley
30 ml (2 tbsp) diced garlic

Place all ingredients in medium to large soup pot and bring to the boil on high heat.

Reduce heat and simmer, covered, for two hours.

Hugh's Buffalo

Serves 12

1 3/4 L (7 c) buffalo or beef stock
1 1/2 kg (3 lbs) cooked buffalo meat diced into 1 cm (1/2 in) cubes
230 g (1/2 lb) double-smoked bacon diced into 1 cm (1/2 in) cubes
30 g (1 oz) dried porcini mushrooms
5 ml (1 tsp) diced garlic

5 ml (1 tsp) red current jelly
240 ml (1 c) onions
5 ml (1 tsp) diced fresh rosemary
5 ml (1 tsp) diced fresh thyme
120 ml (4 oz) chili sauce
240 ml (1 c) roux
120 ml (4 oz) Port wine

Add all ingredients to medium soup pot except roux and Port.

Place on the stove on high and bring to a boil.

Reduce heat and simmer for 10 minutes.

Turn stove back up to high and whisk in roux.

Add Port and serve.

Oyster Mushroom Salsa
Serves 8

120 ml (1/2 c) olive oil
20 oyster mushrooms sliced
120 ml (1/2 c) diced onions
60 g (2 oz) diced garlic
120 ml (1/2 c) diced green peppers
1 jalapeno pepper diced
5 ml (1 tsp) dried oregano
1 1/2 L (6 c) tomato sauce
Juice from **1** lemon
120 ml (1/2 c) chopped coriander

Place oil in a medium-sized soup pot on high heat.

When oil gets hot, add mushrooms, onions, garlic and peppers and cook on high heat while stirring for 10 to 12 minutes.

Add oregano, tomato sauce, lemon juice and coriander.

Bring to the boil. Reduce and simmer 8 to 10 minutes before serving.

Hot Beef Stew
Serves 10

120 ml (1/2 c) olive oil
680 g (1 1/2 lbs) ground beef
1 L (4 c) tomato sauce
240 ml (1 c) diced onions
120 ml (1/2 c) diced leeks
120 ml (1/2 c) diced green peppers
1 large Scotch bonnet pepper diced
2 cloves garlic diced
90 ml (3 oz) chili sauce
30 g (1 oz) chopped oregano
60 g (2 oz) goat cheese

Place oil in medium-sized soup pot on high heat.

Add beef and brown while stirring.

When beef is brown, add all other ingredients except cheese and bring to the boil.

Reduce heat and simmer uncovered for 20 minutes.

Just before serving, stir in cheese.

French Leek
Serves 12

120 ml (1/2 c) vegetable oil
2 L (8 c) sliced leeks
30 ml (2 tbsp) minced garlic
5 ml (1 tsp) fresh thyme diced
6 juniper berries
60 ml (4 tbsp) tomato paste
120 ml (1/2 c) dry sherry
2 1/4 L (9 c) chicken stock
480 ml (2 c) grated Swiss cheese
240 ml (1 c) Romano cheese
10–12 bowl-sized croutons
120 ml (1/2 c) cognac

In a large heavy soup pot, heat oil on high heat.

When oil just begins to smoke, add leeks, garlic and thyme stirring constantly for 8 to 10 minutes – still on high heat.

Add juniper berries and tomato paste while cooking and stirring another 2 minutes.

Deglaze with sherry, add stock, and bring to the boil.

Reduce heat and simmer for 30 minutes.

While soup is simmering, mix both cheeses together.

Preheat over to 200° C (400° F).

Bring soup back to a boil and turn off burner.

Fill individual soup tureens 3/4 full of soup.

Garnish with croutons.

Top off with the cheese mixture.

Place tureens on a baking sheet and put in a 200° C (400° F) oven for 5 to 6 minutes.

Take out of oven. Douse cheese with cognac and serve.

Chicken and Beans
Serves 8

230 g (1/2 lb) raw diced chicken breast, 1 cm (1/2 in) pieces
120 ml (1/2 c) navy beans – dry
240 ml (1 c) diced Spanish onions
60 ml (1/4 c) diced green peppers
60 ml (1/4 c) diced leeks
60 ml (1/4 c) diced celery
60 ml (1/4 c) diced carrots
60 ml (1/4 c) diced smoked bacon
60 ml (1/4 c) sauerkraut
480 ml (2 c) tomato juice
2 cloves garlic diced
4 juniper berries
2 L (8 c) chicken stock – keeping 480 ml (2 c) in reserve

Place all ingredients in a large soup pot and bring to the boil on high heat.

Reduce to medium heat and simmer covered for 2 hours.

If the soup becomes too thick

for your liking, you can add as much of the extra chicken stock as you like.

Return to a boil.

Remove from heat and serve.

Chanterelles with Sun-Dried Tomatoes
Serves 12

60 ml (1/4 c) clarified butter
1 L (4 c) sliced fresh chanterelles
240 ml (1 c) diced Spanish onion
30 ml (2 tbsp) minced garlic
240 ml (1 c) diced leek
480 ml (2 c) diced sun-dried
   tomatoes
5 ml (1 tsp) dried sage
2 L (8 c) chicken stock
90 ml (6 tbsp) buerre-manié
240 ml (1 c) 35% cream
120 ml (1/2 c) white wine

In a medium-sized soup pot, heat butter and add mushrooms, onions, garlic and leeks.

Continue to cook on high, stirring constantly for 6 to 8 minutes.

Add sun-dried tomatoes and sage, cooking for another 2 minutes.

Add chicken stock – still on high – bring to a boil.

Reduce heat to medium and simmer for 10 minutes.

Return to high heat and bring to a boil.

Whisk **240 ml (1 c)** of the boiling stock into the buerre-manié to produce a smooth paste.

Add the smooth paste slowly, while whisking, to the pot of soup.

Add cream and white wine, return to a boil and serve.

Chicken Vegetable
Serves 16

480 ml (2 c) diced onions
240 ml (1 c) diced leek
240 ml (1 c) diced celery
240 ml (1 c) diced carrots
240 ml (1 c) diced red pepper
240 ml (1 c) diced turnip
480 ml (2 c) diced tomatoes
240 ml (1 c) diced parsnips
460 g (1 lb) diced chicken cut
   unto 1 cm (1/2 in) pieces
2 L (8 c) chicken stock
5 ml (1 tsp) Worcestershire sauce

Add all ingredients to a big soup pot.

Bring to a boil on high heat.

Reduce and simmer for 20 minutes before serving.

Calypso Stew
Serves 10

120 ml (1/2 c) vegetable oil
460 g (1 lb) hamburger meat
240 ml (1 c) diced onions
240 ml (1 c) diced green peppers
1 Scotch bonnet pepper diced
120 ml (1/2 c) diced okra
1 large clove of garlic diced
2 anise stars
120 ml (1/2 c) chopped coriander
1 1/4 L (5 c) tomato purée
120 ml (1/2 c) diced mango

Add oil to medium-sized soup pot put on high heat.

When oil begins to smoke, add meat and cook and stir for 4 to 5 minutes.

Add onions, peppers, okra, garlic and anise stars – still on high heat – stirring for 8 to 10 minutes.

Add coriander and cook for 1 more minute while stirring.

Add tomato purée.

Bring to a boil.

Reduce heat and simmer for 5 minutes before serving.

Garnish with chopped mango.

Scampi
Serves 6

115 g (1/4 lb) unsalted butter
6 large scampi cut into
   1/2 cm (1/4 in) pieces
240 ml (1 c) julienne of leeks
5 ml (1 tsp) diced garlic
5 ml (1 tsp) chopped tarragon
120 ml (1/2 c) sun-dried raspberries
60 ml (2 oz) bourbon
1 L (4 c) chicken or fish stock
115 g (4 oz) grated St. Agur cheese

Place butter in medium-sized soup pot on high heat.

Add scampi, leeks, garlic, tarragon and raspberries.

Cook on high heat while stirring for 5 to 6 minutes.

Add bourbon and flambé.

Add stock.

Return to the boil, whisk in cheese and serve.

Rare Steak
Serves 6

2 460-g (1-lb) New York steaks
120 ml (4 oz) olive oil
120 ml (1/2 c) sliced onions
30 ml (2 tbsp) sliced garlic
240 ml (1 c) sliced mushrooms

60 ml (2 oz) brandy
60 ml (2 oz) Grand Marnier
60 ml (2 oz) chili sauce
30 ml (2 tbsp) green peppercorns
    in brine
240 ml (1 c) beef stock
1 L (4 c) demi-glace
60 g (2 oz) whole butter

Salt and pepper the steak.

Heat **60 ml (2 oz)** oil in deep frying pan on high.

When oil begins to smoke, add the steaks, cooking 60 seconds a side.

Remove steaks, leaving the pan on high and adding the other **60 ml (2 oz)** oil, the onions, garlic and mushrooms and cook for 2 minutes while stirring constantly.

Add brandy to the demi-glace and flambé.

Still on high heat, add Grand Marnier, chili sauce, peppercorns with brine and cook while stirring for 60 seconds.

Add beef stock and demi-glace.

Bring to the boil.

Add butter and stir it into the soup, plus the drippings from the steaks.

Cut steaks into **1/2 cm (1/4 in)** strips and place the steak strips into large soup bowls.

Pour soup over meat and serve.

Note: Steak will be, and should be, rare.

Beef Shiitaki
Serves 10

60 ml (1/4 c) peanut oil
680 g (1 1/2 lbs) sirloin steak
    cut into **1 cm (1/2 in)** cubes
240 ml (1 c) sliced onions
240 ml (1 c) sliced red peppers
240 ml (1 c) sliced leeks
360 ml (1 1/2 c) sliced Shiitaki
    mushrooms − 1/2 the stem
    removed
30 ml (2 tbsp) diced garlic
240 ml (1 c) snow peas
1 1/2 L (6 c) beef stock
120 ml (1/2 c) "whitewash"
    (equal parts cornstarch and water)
120 ml (1/2 c) Hoisin sauce

Place oil in medium-sized soup pot on high heat.

When it is red-hot, add beef and cook while stirring for 3 to 4 minutes.

Add onions, peppers, leeks, mushrooms, garlic and snow peas.

Still on high heat, cook while stirring for 4 to 5 minutes.

Add beef stock and bring to the boil.

When the soup comes to a rolling boil, add the "whitewash" mixture.

Add Hoisin sauce and serve.

Chilled Raspberry with Ricotta
Serves 8

1 L (4 c) fresh raspberries crushed
480 ml (2 c) ricotta cheese
240 ml (1 c) dry sherry
480 ml (2 c) 18% cream
120 ml (1/2 c) raspberry jam
30 ml (2 tbsp) fresh dill chopped fine
5 ml (1 tsp) salt
5 ml (1 tsp) nutmeg

Add all ingredients into a large mixing bowl and whisk together well.

Refrigerate for approximately 2 hours and serve.

Roasted Garlic with Tomatoes
Serves 10

50 whole elephant garlic cloves
120 ml (1/2 c) extra virgin olive oil
240 ml (1 c) diced onions
240 ml (1 c) diced green pepper
6 crushed fennel seeds
2 L (8 c) crushed canned tomatoes
5 ml (1 tsp) fresh oregano chopped

In a shallow roasting pan, place whole garlic (basted with oil and salted) into the oven and bake at 180° C (350° F) for 15 to 20 minutes, or until golden brown.

Set garlic aside to skin when cooled.

Add all other ingredients into a large soup pot and place on high heat.

Bring to a boil briefly, then reduce to simmer covered for 8 to 10 minutes.

Mash skinned, roasted garlic, whisk into soup and return to the boil before serving.

Mad About Mushrooms
Serves 10

240 ml (1 c) diced onions
2 large cloves of garlic diced
480 ml (2 c) sliced button
  mushrooms
240 ml (1 c) sliced oyster mushrooms
240 ml (1 c) sliced chanterelle
  mushrooms
120 ml (1/2 c) sliced morel
  mushrooms
30 ml (2 tbsp) diced red pepper
30 ml (2 tbsp) diced fresh sage
30 ml (2 tbsp) tomato paste
2 L (8 c) beef stock
90 ml (6 tbsp) white roux

Put all ingredients except roux in a soup pot and place on high heat.

Bring to the boil then, reduce heat, and simmer for 20 minutes.

Turn back up to a boil and work in the roux.

Boil for 2 minutes more, then serve.

Spanish Vegetable
Serves 8

240 ml (1 c) hot or sweet peppers diced
240 ml (1 c) diced onions
240 ml (1 c) diced carrots
240 ml (1 c) diced celery
240 ml (1 c) diced fennel
120 ml (1/2 c) diced turnip
45 ml (3 tbsp) diced garlic
240 ml (1 c) sliced cabbage
3 diced plum tomatoes
480 ml (2 c) vegetable stock
60 ml (1/4 c) chili sauce
1 bunch fresh coriander chopped

Add all ingredients, except coriander, to a large soup pot and place on medium high heat.

Bring to the boil, while stirring occasionally.

Reduce heat and simmer uncovered for 30 to 40 minutes.

Return to high heat, add coriander, and return to the boil before serving.

Tuscan Bean
Serves 12

(Beans should be soaked for 8 to 12 hours, then cooked in water on medium-high heat for 1 1/2 to 2 hours.)

720 ml (3 c) fully cooked Tuscan beans
60 g (2 oz) butter
240 ml (1 c) diced onions
60 ml (1/4 c) finely diced carrots
480 ml (2 c) double-smoked side bacon cut into small cubes
240 ml (1 c) diced celery
2 cloves garlic diced
5 ml (1 tsp) diced fresh rosemary
240 ml (1 c) mixed red and green peppers chopped
2 L (8 c) ham stock
60 ml (1/4 c) demerara sugar

Melt butter in a hot soup pot, adding onions, carrots, bacon, celery, garlic, beans, rosemary and peppers.

Sauté at high temperature 5 to 6 minutes while stirring constantly.

Add stock and sugar.

Bring to boil and serve.

Swiss Meatball
Serves 14

Meatballs

230 g (1/2 lb) ground beef
230 g (1/2 lb) ground pork
5 ml (1 tsp) diced, fresh garlic
1 egg
30 ml (2 tbsp) bread crumbs
5 ml (1 tsp) powdered beef base
60 ml (1/4 c) diced onions

Mix all ingredients together well in a bowl.

Make **2 1/2 cm (1 in)** round meatballs – put them on an oiled baking tray with a small lip to catch the grease.

Preheat oven to 200° C (400° F) and cook for 10 to 20 minutes.

Soup

115 g (4 oz) double-smoked pork sliced into **1/2 cm (1/4 in)** pieces
240 ml (1 c) diced leeks
240 ml (1 c) diced onions
5 ml (1 tsp) diced garlic
240 ml (1 c) diced celery
240 ml (1 c) diced carrots
120 ml (1/2 c) diced turnips
8 juniper berries
30 ml (2 tbsp) chopped fresh rosemary
240 ml (1 c) sauerkraut
2 L (8 c) veal or chicken stock

With the meatballs put aside, put all ingredients into a medium-sized soup pot and bring to the boil on high heat.

Reduce the heat and simmer for 35 to 40 minutes.

Return to a boil and add meatballs.

Cook for 5 minutes and serve.

Cream of Zucchini Flowers
Serves 8

2 L (8 c) chicken stock
240 ml (1 c) diced onions
5 ml (1 tsp) minced garlic
1 L (4 c) sliced zucchini flowers, stems removed
120 ml (1/2 c) diced roasted red pepper
5 ml (1 tsp) diced fresh tarragon
90 ml (6 tbsp) beurre-manié
240 ml (1 c) shredded St. Agur cheese

Into a large soup pot on high heat, add stock, onions, garlic, zucchini flowers and peppers.

Bring to the boil.

Add tarragon.

In a large bowl, slowly add about **480 ml (2 c)** of the boiling soup to the beurre-manié, whisking until it becomes a smooth paste.

Add the paste to the boiling soup, slowly, still whisking.

Whisk in the cheese.

Return to the boil before serving.

Hungarian Village
Serves 8

60 ml (2 oz) oil
460 g (1 lb) medium ground beef
120 ml (1/2 c) diced leeks
120 ml (1/2 c) diced celery
60 ml (1/4 c) chopped parsnip
120 ml (1/2 c) chopped carrots
120 ml (1/2 c) diced onions
60 ml (1/4 c) diced green pepper
5 ml (1 tsp) chopped garlic
240 ml (1 c) sliced savoy cabbage
5 ml (1 tsp) chopped fresh sage
240 ml (1 c) white wine sauerkraut
30 ml (2 tbsp) sun-dried tomatoes
1 1 1/2-L (48-oz) can tomato juice
2 1/2 L (10 c) chicken stock
45 ml (3 tbsp) beef soup base
5 ml (1 tsp) salt
30 ml (2 tbsp) white sugar

Put oil in your soup pot on high heat.

When oil just begins to smoke, add meat and cook, while stirring, until meat turns completely brown.

Add all vegetables and cook another 4 to 5 minutes

Add sage and sauerkraut and sun-dried tomatoes and cook for 2 more minutes.

Add tomato juice, chicken stock and beef base.

Add salt and sugar.

Bring soup to the boil, reducing to a simmer for 20 minutes.

Clam-Tomato-Garlic
Serves 8

120 ml (1/2 c) extra virgin olive oil
240 ml (1 c) diced onions
120 ml (1/2 c) chopped garlic
240 ml (1 c) diced leeks
60 ml (1/4 c) diced fennel
2 L (8 c) tomato concassée
2 bay leaves
60 ml (1/4 c) chopped fresh oregano
680 g (1 1/2 lbs) clams
120 ml (1/2 c) diced sun-dried tomatoes

Put oil, onions, garlic, leeks and fennel into a large soup pot on high heat.

Cook until garlic goes brown

Add tomatoes concassée, bay leaves and oregano and bring to a boil.

Reduce heat and simmer for 20 minutes.

Add clams and sun-dried tomatoes.

Cover and cook gently for 15 to 20 minutes, stirring occasionally to see if clams are open.

Salt and pepper to taste and serve.

Chilled Raspberry with Bittersweet Chocolate and Lox

Serves 6

120 ml (1/2 c) chopped bittersweet chocolate
120 ml (1/2 c) sour cream
120 ml (1/2 c) raspberry yogurt
360 ml (1 1/2 c) frozen raspberries with syrup
240 ml (1 c) fresh raspberries
1 egg yolk
115 g (4 oz) julienned smoked salmon
480 ml (2 c) 18% cream
1 L (4 c) homogenized milk
Zest of 1 lemon
30 ml (2 tbsp) diced fresh mint
2 ml (1/2 tsp) salt
5 ml (1 tsp) white sugar

Mix all the ingredients in a bowl.

Whisk together well and chill for at least 1 hour.

Summer Lobster

Serves 12

240 ml (1 c) diced red peppers
240 ml (1 c) diced Spanish onion
240 ml (1 c) diced leeks
1 medium-sized jalapeno pepper
240 ml (1 c) sliced mushrooms

2 L (8 c) peeled, seeded and chopped fresh tomatoes
240 ml (1 c) lobster or fish stock
60 ml (2 oz) balsamic vinegar
60 g (2 oz) brown sugar
240 ml (1 c) diced celery
120 ml (1/2 c) chopped fresh coriander
30 ml (2 tbsp) salt
720 ml (3 c) raw lobster meat diced into 2 1/2 cm (1 in) pieces

Place all ingredients, except lobster meat, into a large soup pot, place on high heat and stir.

Bring soup to a boil, stirring occasionally.

Reduce heat and simmer for 25 to 30 minutes.

Add lobster meat and return to the boil for 4 to 5 minutes.

Smoked Turkey Florentine with Stilton

Serves 8

20 ml (1 oz) cooking oil
680 g (1 1/2 lbs) smoked turkey meat cut into 1 cm (1/2 in) pieces
60 ml (1/4 c) onions chopped
30 ml (2 tbsp) diced red pimentos
30 ml (2 tbsp) diced leeks
2 ml (1/2 tsp) diced garlic
30 ml (2 tbsp) freshly chopped tarragon
30 ml (1 oz) dry sherry
1 1/2 L (6 c) turkey or chicken stock

140 g (5 oz) chopped raw spinach
120 ml (1/2 c) white roux
60 ml (2 tbsp) chicken soup base
90 g (3 oz) grated Stilton
5 ml (1 tsp) white sugar
480 ml (2 c) 35% cream

Put oil in your soup pot on high heat, adding turkey, onions, pimentos, leeks, garlic and tarragon when oil just begins to smoke.

Stir on high heat for 4 to 5 minutes.

Deglaze pot with sherry, and add stock.

Bring to the boil and add the spinach, cooking for 2 to 3 minutes.

Whisk in roux and chicken base.

Whisk in cheese until completely dissolved.

Add sugar and cream.

Return to the boil before serving.

Chicken and Corn Chili with Black Beans
Serves 8

60 ml (2 oz) vegetable oil
460 g (1 lb) sliced chicken breast
5 ml (1 tsp) diced garlic
240 ml (1 c) diced green pepper
240 ml (1 c) diced Spanish onion
240 ml (1 c) fresh corn kernels

5 ml (1 tsp) chopped fresh rosemary
5 ml (1 tsp) chopped fresh coriander
60 ml (4 tbsp) chili powder
5 ml (1 tsp) diced sun-dried tomatoes
5 ml (1 tsp) Hoisin sauce
1 1 1/2-L (48-oz) can crushed plum tomatoes
120 ml (1/2 c) chili sauce
240 ml (1 c) tomato juice
30 ml (2 tbsp) chicken soup base
1 600-ml (20-oz) can black beans (with juice)

Add oil to a large soup pot on high heat and as oil just begins to smoke add chicken, garlic, peppers, onions and corn.

Cook on high heat, 4 to 5 minutes while stirring.

Add all herbs including chili powder and sun-dried tomatoes and cook while stirring another 2 minutes.

Add Hoisin sauce, plum tomatoes, chili sauce and tomato juice plus chicken base.

Bring to a boil, then reduce heat to simmer and cook 10 to 12 minutes more.

Add black beans and juice.

Return to the boil before serving.

Curried Chicken

Serves 8

1 L (4 c) chicken stock
480 ml (2 c) cubed cooked chicken
120 ml (1/2 c) diced celery
120 ml (1/2 c) diced onions
120 ml (1/2 c) diced green peppers
5 ml (1 tsp) diced garlic
120 ml (1/2 c) tomato purée
5 ml (1 tsp) dark soy sauce
1 Macintosh apple diced, skin on
80 ml (1/3 c) raw long grain rice
45 ml (3 tbsp) curry powder

Put all ingredients in a medium-sized soup pot on high heat and bring to a boil.

Reduce heat and simmer for 20 minutes before serving.

Lobster Bisque

Serves 4 – 6

60 ml (1/4 c) butter
240 ml (1 c) finely chopped onion
240 ml (1 c) sliced mushrooms
30 ml (2 tbsp) finely diced sweet red peppers or pimento
1 ml (1/4 tsp) dried tarragon
45 ml (3 tbsp) all-purpose flour
1 1/2 L (6 c) lobster stock
5 ml (1 tsp) Armagnac
5 ml (1 tsp) dry sherry

60 ml (1/4 c) 35% cream
480 ml (2 c) lobster meat (frozen lobster tails are ideal for this recipe)

Heat butter in a heavy soup pot over medium-high heat.

Add onions, mushrooms, red pepper and tarragon, sweating until onion becomes translucent.

Whisk in flour to make a white roux and cook about 1 minute.

Slowly whisk in lobster stock – **120 ml (1/2 c)** at a time – until smooth and simmer until slightly thickened.

Stir in Armagnac, sherry, cream, and chopped up lobster meat.

Smoked Chicken with White Grapes

Serves 12

2 L (8 c) chicken stock
480 ml (2 c) smoked chicken breast, coarsely diced
120 ml (1/2 c) finely diced onion
60 ml (1/4 c) finely diced white leek
5 ml (1 tsp) finely diced fresh pimento pepper
1 clove garlic finely diced
5 ml (1 tsp) finely diced sun-dried tomatoes
2 ml (1/2 tsp) dried tarragon
240 ml (1 c) light roux
60 ml (2 oz) 35% cream

30 ml (2 tbsp) white sugar
480 ml (2 c) seedless wine grapes
Sherry (optional)

Put chicken stock, chicken, onions, leeks, peppers, garlic, sun-dried tomatoes and herbs in a large soup pot and bring to the boil.

Boil 4 to 5 minutes, just enough to make vegetables tender but not to overcook the chicken.

Whisk in the roux.

Add 35% cream and sugar, and sherry if desired, bring to a boil, and add grapes. Let sit 2 minutes before serving.

Daring Darrel's Tomato and Carrot
Serves 8

6 large, peeled, seeded and diced tomatoes
240 ml (1 c) fine diced onions
240 ml (1 c) shredded carrots
120 ml (1/2 c) roasted diced garlic*
240 ml (1 c) roasted diced red peppers*
5 ml (1 tsp) chopped fresh oregano
240 ml (1 c) vegetable stock

Roast garlic and peppers in a small roasting pan in olive oil at 200 °C (400° F) until golden brown.

Put all ingredients into a heavy soup pot and place on high heat.

Bring to a boil.

Reduce heat and simmer for 20 minutes, stirring occasionally.

Smoked Chicken "Yanna"
Serves 10

115 g (1/4 lb) butter
240 ml (1 c) diced onions
2 large cloves of garlic sliced
680 g (1 1/2 lbs) smoked chicken, diced into 1 cm (1/2 in) pieces
240 ml (1 c) grilled sliced pimento pepper
115 g (4 oz) smoked salmon julienne
4 strings saffron
60 ml (4 tbsp) cooked wild rice
1 1/2 L (6 c) chicken stock
240 ml (1 c) julienne sliced prosciutto

Put butter in a medium-sized soup pot on high and heat until butter begins to froth.

Add onions and garlic and keep on high until onions and garlic are golden brown.

Add all other ingredients except the prosciutto.

Bring to a boil before serving.

Garnish the top of each serving with prosciutto.

Last Night's Leg of Lamb
Serves 8

480 ml (2 c) cooked lamb diced
  into **1 cm (1/2 in)** cubes
120 ml (1/2 c) diced onions
120 ml (1/2 c) diced green peppers
120 ml (1/2 c) diced leeks
120 ml (1/2 c) diced carrots
30 ml (2 tbsp) diced garlic
5 ml (1 tsp) fresh chopped rosemary
45 ml (3 tbsp) tomato paste
120 ml (1/2 c) penne regatta
1 1/4 L (5 c) lamb or beef stock

Put all ingredients in medium-sized soup pot and put on high heat. Bring to a boil. Reduce and simmer for 20 minutes. Serve.

Asparagus Parmesan
Serves 12

1 1/2 L (6 c) chicken or vegetable
  stock
1 L (4 c) chopped asparagus
240 ml (1 c) diced onions
240 ml (1 c) diced green peppers
240 ml (1 c) diced leeks
5 ml (1 tsp) diced garlic
5 ml (1 tsp) chopped sun-dried
  tomatoes
6 large eggs

240 ml (1 c) grated Parmesan
60 ml (1/4 c) cooked long grain rice

Put stock, asparagus, onions, peppers, leeks, garlic and sun-dried tomatoes in a medium-sized soup pot on high heat and bring to a boil for 6 to 8 minutes.

While this is boiling, mix eggs and cheese together until it forms a paste.

With soup still at the boil, whisk eggs and cheese mixture into the soup.

Add rice and return to the boil before serving.

Mussel Pesto
Serves 8

60 ml (1/4 c) clarified butter
120 ml (1/2 c) diced onions
45 ml (3 tbsp) diced fresh garlic
1 1/2 L (6 c) fish stock
240 ml (1 c) fresh basil chopped
460 g (1 lb) live mussels
240 ml (1 c) roasted pine nuts
  for garnish

Melt butter in medium-sized soup pot.

Add onions and garlic cooking on high heat while stirring constantly for 5 to 6 minutes.

Add stock and basil and bring to a boil.

Add mussels and cover for 6 to 10 minutes to open mussels.

Using a slotted spoon, place an equal number of mussels in each bowl and pour soup over the mussels.

Garnish with pine nuts.

Lobster Basmati
Serves 8

60 ml (1/4 c) clarified butter
460 g (1 lb) raw lobster meat
   chopped into **1 cm (1/2 in)** pieces
2 large cloves of garlic diced
240 ml (1 c) diced onions
240 ml (1 c) finely diced red peppers
120 ml (1/2 c) Basmati rice
240 ml (1 c) diced leeks
45 ml (3 tbsp) curry powder
1 L (4 c) chicken or fish stock
30 ml (1 oz) mushroom soy sauce
60 ml (2 oz) mango chutney

Pre-heat medium-sized soup pot on high heat and add butter.

When hot, add lobster, garlic, onions, peppers, rice and leeks, stirring on high heat for 6 to 8 minutes.

Stir in curry powder, add stock and bring to the boil.

Reduce heat and let simmer uncovered for 15 to 20 minutes.

Stir in soy sauce and chutney.

Chipolata Sausage
Serves 8

120 ml (1/2 c) virgin olive oil
240 ml (1 c) onions julienne
30 ml (2 tbsp) diced fresh garlic
120 ml (1/2 c) diced fresh fennel
120 ml (1/2 c) diced green peppers
240 ml (1 c) sliced oyster
   mushrooms
480 ml (2 c) cooked chipolata
   sausage sliced into
   1/2 cm (1/4 in) medallions
1 1/2 L (6 c) crushed, canned plum
   tomatoes
120 ml (1/2 c) cooked long
   grain rice

Add oil to a medium-sized soup pot on high heat.

When oil begins to smoke, add onion, garlic, fennel, peppers and mushrooms, stirring frequently for 8 to 10 minutes.

Add sausage and cook another 1 minute.

Add tomatoes and rice.

Bring to a boil briefly, reduce heat to simmer for 2 minutes and add rice.

Sirloin and Oysters
Serves 10

460 g (1 lb) rare sirloin steak
cut into **1 cm (1/2 in)** cubes
60 ml (1/4 c) clarified butter
240 ml (1 c) diced onions
45 ml (3 tbsp) diced fresh garlic
120 ml (1/2 c) diced red peppers
6 large, grilled portobello
mushrooms, sliced
60 ml (1/4 c) tomato paste
1 1/2 L (6 c) beef stock
240 ml (1 c) white wine
60 g (2 oz) fresh tarragon diced
80 ml (1/3 c) roux
24 freshly shucked oysters
with juice

Grill steak at high temperature
until browned but rare before
cutting into cubes.

Melt butter in medium-sized soup
pot on high heat.

Add onions, garlic, peppers and
mushrooms, stirring constantly
for 10 to 12 minutes.

Add tomato paste and cook
another 2 minutes while stirring.

Add beef stock, wine and tarragon
and bring to a boil.

Reduce heat and simmer for
5 minutes.

Bring soup back to the boil and
whisk roux into the soup very
slowly.

Add oysters.

Return briefly to the boil.

Place an equal serving of cubed
sirloin into serving bowls. Pour
hot soup over rare sirloin and
serve.

Pike Bisque
Serves 10 – 12

60 ml (1/4 c) whole butter
680 g (1 1/2 lbs) skinned pike meat
cut into **1 cm (1/2 in)** pieces
240 ml (1 c) diced onions
240 ml (1 c) diced green of leeks
5 ml (1 tsp) diced garlic
30 ml (2 tbsp) tomato paste
5 ml (1 tsp) chopped fresh tarragon
30 ml (2 tbsp) green peppercorns
in brine
30 ml (1 oz) bourbon
30 ml (1 oz) lemon juice
1 1/2 L (6 c) fish stock
100 ml (7 tbsp) white roux

Place butter in medium-sized
soup pot on high heat.

When butter begins to froth,
add pike, onions, leeks and garlic
and cook on high heat for 5 to
6 minutes while stirring.

Add tomato paste, tarragon,
and peppercorns and cook for
2 minutes.

Add bourbon, lemon juice,
and stock.

Bring to a rolling boil and slowly whisk in roux.

Quail with Cherries
Serves 10

Roast **6** quail in the oven at 180° C (350° F) for 25 to 30 minutes. Remove from oven and place them in a pot with **2 1/2 L (10 c)** of boiling water. Deglaze the pan in which you cooked the quail and add renderings into the pot as well.

Bring to a boil.

Reduce heat to simmer for 50 to 60 minutes, then strain liquid into another pot.

Place quail in the refrigerator until cool enough to pick meat from bones and chop into small pieces.

90 ml (3 oz) clarified butter
480 ml (2 c) diced onion
240 ml (1 c) julienne of green leeks
30 ml (2 tbsp) diced garlic
60 ml (1/4 c) wild rice
30 ml (2 tbsp) julienne of orange rind
240 ml (1 c) julienne of roast pimento
60 ml (1/4 c) red current jelly
2 L (8 c) quail stock
720 ml (3 c) pitted half cherries
90 ml (3 oz) Cassis

Into a medium-sized soup pot on high heat, add butter, onions, leeks, garlic and rice and cook for 4 to 5 minutes while stirring.

Add quail meat, orange rind, pimento and jelly and cook for 1 minute more on high heat while stirring.

Add stock, and bring to a boil.

Add cherries, Cassis, reduce heat and simmer for 35 to 40 minutes.

Tomato Tomato
Serves 8

60 ml (1/4 c) olive oil
240 ml (1 c) finely diced onions
3 large cloves of garlic diced
240 ml (1 c) finely diced green peppers
480 ml (2 c) sun-dried tomatoes
1 1/2 L (6 c) tomato purée
120 ml 1/2 c) diced fresh oregano

Add onions, garlic and peppers to oil in a small soup pot on medium heat and sweat for 6 to 8 minutes while stirring gently.

Add sun-dried tomatoes and cook for 2 minutes more.

Add tomato purée and oregano.

Bring the soup to the boil, reduce heat and simmer for 8 to 10 minutes.

Lobster Mornay

Serves 10

60 ml (4 tbsp) clarified butter
240 ml (1 c) diced onions
5 ml (1 tsp) diced garlic
5 ml (1 tsp) chopped fresh tarragon
30 ml (2 tbsp) Spanish paprika
240 ml (1 c) sliced chanterelle
    mushrooms
120 ml (1/2 c) Armagnac
1 3/4 L (7 c) lobster or fish stock
75 ml (5 tbsp) buerre-manié
60 ml (1/4 c) diced lobster meat
    cut into **1 cm (1/2 in)** pieces
230 g (1/2 lb) grated Swiss cheese
120 ml (1/2 c) grated Parmesan
240 ml (1 c) 35% cream

Add butter to a medium-sized soup pot and put on high heat.

When butter begins to brown, add onions, garlic, tarragon, paprika and mushrooms and cook on high for 4 to 5 minutes.

Add Armagnac and flambé.

Add stock to the mixture.

In a medium-sized bowl make buerre-manié.

Pour about **480 ml (2 c)** of the soup into the buerre-manié and whisk until it becomes a smooth paste.

Add the paste back into the soup slowly while whisking, add lobster meat and return to the boil.

Whisk in cheeses until completely melted.

Add cream and serve.

Italian Rib

Serves 12

680 g (1 1/2 lbs) side ribs cut into
    5 cm (2 in) racks against the bone
60 ml (1/4 c) olive oil
240 ml (1 c) diced leeks
240 ml (1 c) diced onions
240 ml (1 c) diced fennel
240 ml (1 c) diced green peppers
10 ml (2 tsp) diced garlic
5 ml (1 tsp) dried oregano
10 ml (2 tsp) crushed dried porcini
    mushrooms
5 ml (1 tsp) crushed dried chilies
2 1/2 L (10 c) tomato concassée

Put ribs on a baking sheet and bake for 15 to 20 minutes at 200°C (400° F).

Remove and let cool.

Put oil in a medium-sized soup pot on high heat. Add leeks, onions, fennel, green peppers, garlic and cook, stirring, for 5 to 6 minutes.

Add oregano, mushrooms and chilies and cook another 2 minutes.

Add tomato concassée and bring to a boil before reducing to low heat.

When meat has cooled, separate the ribs and drop them into the soup.

Simmer for 25 to 30 minutes, stirring occasionally.

Return to the boil before serving.

Spanish Crab
Serves 10

60 ml (1/4 c) olive oil
2 garlic cloves minced
120 ml (1/2 c) diced onions
120 ml (1/2 c) diced green peppers
60 ml (2 tbsp) diced jalapeno
120 ml (1/2 c) diced leeks
120 ml (1/2 c) chopped fresh
   coriander
900 g (2 lbs) snow crab
1 1/2 L (6 c) crushed tomatoes

Heat oil in large soup pot on high heat.

When oil just begins to smoke, add garlic, onions, peppers and leeks and cook on high for 6 to 8 minutes, stirring constantly.

Add coriander and crabmeat and stir for 2 minutes.

Add tomato, still on high, stirring until it reaches a boil.

Reduce heat immediately and simmer for 5 to 8 minutes.

Oxtail and Beans
Serves 6

1 1/2 kg (3 lbs) browned oxtails
2 3/4 L (11 c) mild beef stock
240 ml (1 c) dried white beans
4 cloves of garlic diced
240 ml (1 c) onions
120 ml (1/2 c) diced turnip
120 ml (1/2 c) diced carrots
120 ml (1/2 c) diced parsnips
60 ml (1/4 c) sun-dried tomatoes
240 ml (1 c) sauerkraut
5 ml (1 tsp) freshly chopped
   rosemary
2 bay leaves

To brown oxtails:

Salt and pepper the oxtails. Put them on a baking sheet in a 200° C (400° F) oven for 40 to 60 minutes.

Put all ingredients, including oxtails, in a large soup pot on high heat. Bring to a boil.

Reduce to simmer for 2 1/2 to 3 hours or until meat starts coming away from the bones.

Remove oxtails from soup with slotted spoon and remove meat from bones.

Add the meat back to the stock.

Return to a boil and serve.

Cream of Onion and Garlic
Serves 10 – 12

60 ml (1/4 c) unsalted butter
240 ml (1 c) finely diced leeks
1 1/4 L (5 c) finely diced Spanish
   onions (about **2 1/2** large onions)
45 ml (3 tbsp) minced garlic
   (about **9** cloves)
30 ml (2 tbsp) diced pimento or
   sweet red pepper
120 ml (1/2 c) dry white wine
2 L (8 c) chicken stock
5 ml (1 tsp) Worcestershire sauce
5 ml (1 tsp) granulated white sugar
75 ml (5 tbsp) buerre-manié
240 ml (1 c) 35% cream
120 ml (1/2 c) chicken base
5 ml (1 tsp) dry mustard
2 ml (1/2 tsp) ground nutmeg
Salt to taste
White pepper to taste

In a large, heavy soup pot, melt butter over high heat until butter begins to turn a nutty brown color.

Add leek and onions; cook over high heat, stirring constantly for 3 or 4 minutes or until onion has softened.

Add garlic and pimento, continue to cook 2 minutes, stirring constantly.

Reduce heat to medium-high, add wine, chicken stock, Worcestershire sauce and sugar.

Bring to a boil, reduce heat to medium, and simmer for 5 to 10 minutes.

In a medium-sized bowl, whisk beurre-manié until smooth.

Slowly whisk in **240 ml (1 c)** of the soup mixture until beurre-manié resembles a smooth paste. Whisk into the soup 1 spoonful at a time, stirring constantly.

Simmer gently to thicken slightly.

Stir in cream and season with base, mustard, nutmeg, salt and pepper. Bring just to a boil and ladle into soup bowls.

Smoked Turkey with Cheshire
Serves 8

60 ml (1/4 c) clarified butter
120 ml (1/2 c) diced onions
5 ml (1 tsp) diced garlic
680 g (1 1/2 lbs) diced double-
   smoked turkey cut into
   1 cm (1/2 in) pieces
5 ml (1 tsp) chopped fresh sage
1 L (4 c) chicken or turkey stock
2 Belgian endives shredded thin
115 g (1/4 lb) shredded Cheshire
   cheese

Put butter in a medium-sized soup pot on high heat.

Add onions and garlic and sweat for 4 to 5 minutes while stirring.

Add turkey and sage and cook for another 2 minutes.

Add stock, bring to the boil and add endive.

After the endive is stirred in well, whisk in cheese before serving.

Stracciatella
Serves 10 – 12

60 ml (1/4 c) unsalted butter
480 ml (2 c) chopped onion
    (about 1 large)
240 ml (1 c) sliced leek
    (about 1 large)
2 ml (1/2 tsp) minced garlic
240 ml (1 c) finely sliced carrots
    (about 2 medium)
240 ml (1 c) sliced mushrooms
720 ml (3 c) sliced zucchini
    (about 3 small)
1 head of broccoli, coarsely chopped
1 240 ml (1 c) diced green pepper
    (about 1 medium)
720 ml (3 c) tomatoes, diced
    (about 3 medium)
5 ml (1 tsp) dried oregano
1 3/4 L (7 c) chicken stock
90 g (3 oz) vermicelli noodles,
    broken into 5 cm (2 in) lengths
2 large eggs, beaten
240 ml (1 c) grated Parmesan cheese
60 ml (1/4 c) lemon juice
    (juice of 1 1/2 lemons)
5 ml (1 tsp) Worcestershire sauce
Salt to taste
White pepper to taste

In a large, heavy soup pot, melt butter over medium-high heat.

When butter begins to foam, add onion and leek; sauté 3 to 4 minutes or until vegetables have wilted.

Add garlic and sauté for 1 minute, stirring constantly.

Add carrots, mushrooms, zucchini, broccoli, green pepper, tomatoes, and oregano. Sauté for 10 minutes, but do not brown.

Stir in stock. Bring to a boil, reduce heat to medium and simmer for 15 minutes or until vegetables are tender.

Add noodles and continue to simmer for 10 minutes.

In a medium-sized bowl, beat eggs with a fork until frothy.

Bring soup to a rolling boil, and slowly add eggs to soup while mixing soup continuously.

Add spoonfuls of cheese to soup while mixing continuously.

Season with lemon juice, Worcestershire sauce, salt and pepper.

Cream of Zucchini and Eggplant
Serves 8 – 10

60 ml (1/4 c) unsalted butter
240 ml (1 c) finely diced leeks
240 ml (1 c) finely diced onions
480 ml (2 c) diced zucchini
480 ml (2 c) unpeeled, diced
   eggplant
60 ml (1/4 c) finely diced sweet red
   pepper or pimento
5 ml (1 tsp) minced garlic
   (about 1 medium clove)
2 ml (1/2 tsp) dried tarragon
2 ml (1/2 tsp) chopped fresh basil
60 ml (1/4 c) dry white wine
2 L (8 c) chicken stock
90 ml (6 tbsp) beurre-manié
120 ml (1/2 c) 35% cream
5 ml (1 tsp) Worcestershire sauce
Ground nutmeg to taste
Salt to taste
White pepper to taste

In a large, heavy soup pot, melt butter over medium-high heat until butter turns to a nutty brown color.

Add leeks, onions, zucchini, eggplant, red pepper, and garlic; sweat until vegetables are tender, about 5 minutes.

Stir in tarragon, basil, and wine, bring to a boil, and reduce by half, about 2 to 3 minutes.

Stir in stock, bring to a boil, reduce heat to medium, and simmer for 5 minutes.

In a medium-sized bowl, whisk beurre-manié until smooth. Slowly whisk in **240 ml (1 c)** to **480 ml (2 c)** of the soup mixture until beurre-manié resembles a smooth paste. Whisk into soup, 1 spoonful at a time, whisking constantly. Simmer until soup has thickened slightly.

Bring soup back to a boil, stir in cream, and season with Worcestershire sauce, nutmeg, salt, and pepper. Serve immediately.

French Vegetable and Cheshire Cheese
Serves 10 – 12

60 ml (1/4 c) unsalted butter
720 ml (3 c) diced Spanish onion
480 ml (2 c) diced carrots
240 ml (1 c) sliced leek
480 ml (2 c) chopped celery
720 ml (3 c) coarsely chopped
   zucchini
480 ml (2 c) sliced mushrooms
1 bunch broccoli, coarsely chopped
1 medium green pepper, sliced
480 ml (2 c) diced tomatoes
   (about 2 medium)
2 ml (1/2 tsp) finely diced garlic
30 ml (2 tbsp) dried oregano
2 ml (1/2 tsp) dried basil
5 ml (1 tsp) Worcestershire sauce

5 ml (1 tsp) granulated sugar
2 L (8 c) chicken stock
90 g (3 oz) linguini noodles, broken in threes
230 g (1/2 lb) English Cheshire cheese, grated
Salt to taste
White pepper to taste

In a large, heavy soup pot, melt butter over medium-high heat.

When butter begins to foam slightly, add onion, carrot, leek, and celery.

Sauté for 3 to 4 minutes or until vegetables are slightly wilted.

Add zucchini, mushrooms, broccoli, green pepper, tomatoes, and garlic, and sauté for 3 to 4 minutes.

Add oregano, basil, Worcestershire sauce, and sugar.

Stir in chicken stock, bring to a boil, add noodles, and cook for 7 minutes.

Add a handful of cheese at a time while stirring constantly until melted.

Season with salt and pepper.

Serve immediately.

Oyster Stew
Serves 8 – 10

30 ml (2 tbsp) unsalted butter
120 ml (1/2 c) finely diced onion
120 ml (1/2 c) finely diced leek
2 ml (1/2 tsp) minced garlic
12 fresh oysters, shucked, reserve juice
5 ml (1 tsp) brandy
30 ml (2 tbsp) dry white wine
360 ml (1 1/2 c) 35% cream
2 ml (1/2 tsp) Worcestershire sauce
Ground nutmeg to taste
Salt to taste
White pepper to taste
15 ml (1 tbsp) grated Romano cheese

Heat butter in a medium-sized, heavy saucepan over medium-high heat.

Add onion, leek, and garlic; sweat until onion is transparent and leek is tender, about 3 or 4 minutes.

Add oysters, oyster juice, and brandy.

As soon as brandy is warm, ignite with a match to flambé.

Once flames have died out completely, stir in wine and bring mixture just to a boil.

Stir in cream and season with Worcestershire sauce, nutmeg, salt, and pepper.

Stir in cheese and serve.

Chilled Peanut Butter with Frangelica
Serves 4 – 6

360 ml (1 1/2 c) chunky peanut
butter
240 ml (1 c) sour cream
1 L (4 c) half-and-half cream (10%)
45 ml (3 tbsp) lemon juice
(juice of **1** lemon)
30 ml (2 tbsp) lime juice
(juice of **1** lime)
60 ml (1/4 c) Frangelica liqueur
10 ml (2 tsp) grated lemon rind
7 ml (1 1/2 tsp) grated lime rind
5 ml (1 tsp) granulated sugar
Ground nutmeg to taste
Salt to taste

Place peanut butter in a large
bowl.

Whisk in sour cream, 10% cream,
lemon juice, lime juice, Frangelica,
lemon rind, and lime rind.

Season with sugar, nutmeg,
and salt.

Chill for 12 hours before serving.

Cantonese Braised Beef and Oyster
Serves 8 – 10

60 ml (1/4 c) peanut or vegetable oil
460 g (1 lb) flank steak, diced into
1 cm (1/2 in) cubes
480 ml (2 c) diced Spanish onions
120 ml (1/2 c) diced carrots
240 ml (1 c) diced green peppers
120 ml (1/2 c) sliced mushrooms
5 ml (1 tsp) minced garlic
2 ml (1/2 tsp) Chinese five-spice
powder
5 ml (1 tsp) granulated sugar
1 1/2 L (6 c) beef stock
60 ml (1/4 c) cornstarch
60 ml (1/4 c) cold water
60 ml (1/4 c) oyster sauce
12 fresh oysters, shucked, reserve
juice
Salt to taste
White pepper to taste

In a large heavy soup pot, heat
oil over high heat until a wisp of
smoke appears.

Add meat and sauté for 2 to
3 minutes, stirring constantly.

Add onions, carrots, green
peppers, and mushrooms,
and continue to sauté for 3 or
4 minutes or until vegetables are
tender-crisp.

Stir in garlic, five-spice powder,
and sugar and stock.

Bring to a boil, reduce heat to medium-low and simmer for 10 minutes.

In a small bowl, stir cornstarch with water until combined.

Whisk into soup and continue to simmer for 2 or 3 minutes, or until soup has thickened slightly.

Whisk in oyster sauce, then add oysters and their juice.

Season with salt and pepper and ladle into bowls.

Note: Be sure not to overcook oysters. They take just a few minutes to cook.

Beef with Green Peppers
Serves 10 – 12

120 ml (1/2 c) unsalted butter
900 g (2 lbs) flank steak, diced into
   1 cm (1/2 in) cubes
480 ml (2 c) diced Spanish onion
720 ml (3 c) diced green pepper
   (about 3 medium)
120 ml (1/2 c) diced carrots (about
   1 medium)
5 ml (1 tsp) minced garlic
2 ml (1/2 tsp) dried tarragon
120 ml (1/2 c) dry red wine
60 ml (1/4 c) hard or all-purpose
   flour
2 L (8 c) beef stock
30 ml (2 tbsp) tomato paste
45 ml (3 tbsp) chili sauce

5 ml (1 tsp) Dijon mustard
Salt to taste
Black pepper to taste

In a large soup pot, melt **60 ml (1/4 c)** of butter over medium-high heat until foamy.

Add beef and sauté about 3 or 4 minutes, stirring occasionally until lightly browned.

Add onion, green pepper, carrots, garlic, and tarragon and continue to sauté, stirring frequently, 3 or 4 minutes more, or until onion has wilted.

Stir in red wine, bring to a boil, and reduce to half the amount. Remove to a bowl and set aside. Add the remaining butter to soup pot and melt over medium-high heat.

Stir in flour and continue to cook, stirring constantly, until the flour is golden brown, about 3 or 4 minutes.

While whisking constantly, pour in **120 ml (1/2 c)** of stock at a time until the mixture is smooth and has thickened slightly.

Whisk in tomato paste, chili sauce, and mustard.

Bring to a boil, reduce heat to medium-low, add vegetable and meat mixture, and simmer for 5 or 10 minutes or until vegetables are tender.

Season with salt and pepper and serve.

Sicilian Meatball
Serves 8

Meatballs

230 g (1/2 lb) ground beef
2 ml (1/2 tsp) ground black pepper
2 ml (1/2 tsp) salt
5 ml (1 tsp) Worcestershire sauce
2 ml (1/2 tsp) minced garlic
1 egg slightly beaten
30 ml (2 tbsp) chopped parsley
60 ml (1/4 c) vegetable oil

Combine beef, pepper, salt, Worcestershire sauce, garlic, egg and parsley. Work by hand until thoroughly mixed. Roll into **2 1/2 cm (1 in)** diameter meatballs. There should be about 15 to 20 meatballs.

Soup

60 ml (1/4 c) unsalted butter
360 ml (1 1/2 c) diced Spanish onions
240 ml (1 c) diced green peppers
120 ml (1/2 c) finely diced celery
120 ml (1/2 c) finely diced leek
2 ml (1/2 tsp) minced garlic
2 ml (1/2 tsp) fennel seeds
2 ml (1/2 tsp) dried oregano
10 large tomatoes, peeled, seeded, and chopped
480 ml (2 c) beef stock
Salt to taste
Black pepper to taste

In a large skillet, heat oil over medium-high heat. Add meatballs and brown on all sides.

In a medium-sized heavy soup pot, heat butter over medium-high heat until melted.

Add onions, peppers, celery, leek, and garlic, and sauté for 3 to 4 minutes, stirring occasionally until the vegetables are wilted.

Add fennel, oregano, tomatoes, and stock, and simmer for 15 minutes.

Add meatballs, season with salt and pepper, and serve.

Italian Sausage
Serves 8 – 10

60 ml (1/4 c) unsalted butter
480 ml (2 c) finely diced leeks
240 ml (1 c) finely diced onion
240 ml (1 c) finely diced celery
240 ml (1 c) diced green pepper (about **1** pepper)
5 ml (1 tsp) minced garlic
2 L (8 c) tomatoes, peeled, seeded, and diced (about **8** large)
2 ml (1/2 tsp) oregano
2 ml (1/2 tsp) fennel seeds
5 ml (1 tsp) granulated sugar
1 dried chili pepper, crushed
480 ml (2 c) chicken stock
30 ml (2 tbsp) tomato paste
345 g (3/4 lb) Italian sausage

5 ml (1 tsp) Worcestershire sauce
Salt to taste
White pepper to taste

In a large heavy soup pot, melt butter over medium-high heat.

Add leeks, onions, celery, green pepper, and garlic; sweat until vegetables are tender, about 5 to 6 minutes.

Add tomatoes, oregano, fennel seeds, and sugar, and simmer for 20 minutes.

Stir in chili pepper, chicken stock, tomato paste, and sausages, and continue to cook for 10 to 15 minutes or until sausages are fully cooked.

Remove sausages to a plate and allow to cool, cut into **2 1/2 cm (1 in)** slices and return to soup pot.

Season with Worcestershire sauce, salt, and pepper and serve.

Cajun Clams
Serves 6 – 8

60 ml (1/4 c) unsalted butter
240 ml (1 c) diced green pepper
(about **1** medium)
240 ml (1 c) diced celery
480 ml (2 c) diced Spanish onion
(about **1** large)
120 ml (1/2 c) diced leek
(about **1** small)

5 ml (1 tsp) minced garlic
5 ml (1 tsp) chopped capers
5 ml (1 tsp) dried oregano
5 ml (1 tsp) dried basil
2 ml (1/2 tsp) dried tarragon
60 ml (1/4 c) dry sherry
2 L (8 c) peeled, seeded, and diced tomatoes (about **8** large)
45 ml (3 tbsp) lemon juice
(about **1** lemon)
460 g (1 lb) clams
Salt to taste
White pepper to taste

In a large soup pot, melt butter over medium-high heat until bubbly.

Add green pepper, celery, onion, and leek, and sauté 3 or 4 minutes, stirring occasionally, or until vegetables have wilted slightly.

Add garlic and continue cooking for 30 seconds.

Stir in capers, oregano, basil, tarragon, sherry and tomatoes, and bring to a boil.

Reduce heat to medium-low and simmer for 25 minutes.

After 25 minutes, increase heat to medium-high and return soup to boil.

Add lemon juice and clams and cook covered about 5 minutes or until clams have opened.

Season with salt and white pepper to taste.

Mussel Stew – Café de Paris
Serves 10 – 12

60 ml (1/4 c) unsalted butter
480 ml (2 c) diced onion
    (about 1 large)
480 ml (2 c) diced leeks
    (about 2 medium)
5 ml (1 tsp) minced garlic
    (about 3 medium cloves)
480 ml (2 c) diced green pepper
    (about 2)
5 ml (1 tsp) tarragon
60 ml (1/4 c) brandy
240 ml (1 c) red wine
2 L (8 c) chicken stock
30 ml (2 tbsp) chopped capers
5 ml (1 tsp) diced anchovies
    (about 3 or 4)
60 small mussels, cleaned and
    bearded
5 ml (1 tsp) Worcestershire sauce
5 ml (1 tsp) Pernod
30 ml (2 tbsp) lemon juice
    (from 1/2 lemon)
Salt and white pepper to taste

In a large, heavy soup pot, melt butter over medium-high heat.

Add onion, leeks, and garlic and cook until leeks are wilted, about 3 to 5 minutes, stirring occasionally.

Add green pepper and tarragon, sauté for 1 or 2 minutes or until pepper has softened slightly.

Stir in brandy and red wine. Bring to a boil and reduce liquid by half.

Stir in chicken stock, capers, and anchovies, and return to boil.

Add mussels. Cover and cook about 5 minutes, stirring once, or until mussels have opened.

Season with Worcestershire sauce, Pernod, lemon juice, salt, and pepper.

Mandarin Orange with Lime and Fresh Dill
Serves 6

1 L (4 c) fresh mandarin orange or
    orange juice
60 ml (1/4 c) dry sherry
480 ml (2 c) plain yogurt or sour
    cream
480 ml (2 c) table cream (18%) or
    half and half (10%)
120 ml (1/2 c) lime juice (4 limes)
5 ml (1 tsp) grated lime rind
    (2 limes)
5 ml (1 tsp) chopped fresh dill
Ground nutmeg to taste

Pour mandarin orange or orange juice into a large mixing bowl.

Whisk in sherry, 360 ml (1 1/2 c) yogurt or sour cream, cream, lime juice, and lime rind. Season with dill and nutmeg. Chill for 4 hours.

To serve, ladle into soup bowls and garnish each with a dollop of the remaining **120 ml (1/2 c)** yogurt or sour cream.

Cream of Fresh Basil
Serves 2 – 4

60 ml (1/4 c) unsalted butter
360 ml (1 1/2 c) finely diced onion
240 ml (1 c) finely diced leek
180 ml (3/4 c) chopped fresh basil
80 ml (1/3 c) dry white wine
720 ml (3 c) chicken stock
45 ml (3 tbsp) beurre-manié
60 ml (1/4 c) 35% cream
2 ml (1/2 tsp) dry mustard
Ground nutmeg to taste
Salt to taste
White pepper to taste

In a medium-sized, heavy soup pot, heat butter over medium-high heat.

Add onion, leek, and basil; sweat until onion and leek are limp. Stir in wine, bring to a boil, and reduce to half the amount.

Stir in stock, bring to the boil, reduce heat to medium, and simmer for 5 minutes.

In a medium-sized bowl, whisk beurre-manié until smooth. Slowly whisk in **240 ml (1 c)** of the soup mixture until beurre-manié resembles a smooth paste. Add to the soup 1 spoonful at a time, whisking constantly. Simmer until thickened slightly.

Stir in cream and season with mustard, nutmeg, salt, and pepper to taste and serve.

Pineapple and Kiwi with Sherry
Serves 4 – 6

1 pineapple, peeled and cored
6 kiwis, peeled
540 ml (2 1/4 c) table cream (18%)
60 ml (1/4 c) dry sherry
7 ml (1 1/2 tsp) brandy
5 ml (1 tsp) diced fresh dill
Ground nutmeg to taste

On the large blade of a grater, grate 3/4 of the pineapple and 5 of the kiwis into a medium-sized bowl.

Quarter the remaining pineapple and slice the remaining kiwi and set aside for garnish.

Stir in cream, sherry, and brandy, and season with dill, nutmeg.

Chill at least 4 hours.

To serve, ladle into chilled soup bowls, and garnish with pineapple and kiwi slices.

Cream of Braised Lettuce
Serves 10 – 12

60 ml (1/4 c) unsalted butter
720 ml (3 c) finely diced Spanish
   onions (about 1 1/2 large onions)
480 ml (2 c) finely diced leeks (about
   2 large leeks)
240 ml (1 c) finely diced celery
2 ml (1/2 tsp) minced garlic
120 ml (1/2 c) finely diced pimento
   or sweet red bell pepper
60 ml (1/4 c) dry white wine
5 ml (1 tsp) Worcestershire sauce
1 3/4 L (7 c) chicken stock
1 large leaf lettuce, coarsely chopped
75 ml (5 tbsp) beurre-manié
240 ml (1 c) 35% cream
2 ml (1/2 tsp) ground nutmeg
Salt and white pepper to taste

In a large, heavy soup pot, melt butter over medium-high heat until it is a nutty, light brown color.

Add onions, leeks, and celery; sweat, stirring occasionally until vegetables are limp, about 5 minutes.

Add garlic, pimento, wine and Worcestershire sauce, bring to a boil, and simmer for 2 minutes.

Stir in chicken stock.

Return to boil, add lettuce, and simmer 1 minute.

In a medium-sized bowl, whisk beurre-manié until smooth.

Slowly add **240 ml (1 c)** of the soup mixture, whisking slowly until beurre-manié resembles a smooth paste.

Whisk into the soup mixture 1 spoonful at a time, simmering gently to thicken slightly.

Stir in cream and season with nutmeg, salt, and pepper to taste.

Leek and Endive
in Clear Broth
Serves 10 – 12

60 ml (1/4 c) unsalted butter
720 ml (3 c) diced leek
240 ml (1 c) diced onion
120 ml (1/2 c) finely diced sweet red
   pepper or pimento
120 ml (1/2 c) finely diced green
   pepper
240 ml (1 c) sliced mushrooms
240 ml (1 c) diced celery
5 ml (1 tsp) minced garlic
1 ml (1/4 tsp) dried tarragon
2 ml (1/2 tsp) dried thyme
7 ml (1 1/2 tsp) dried oregano
2 ml (1/2 tsp) fennel seeds
60 ml (1/4 c) dry sherry
240 ml (1 c) tomatoes, peeled,
   seeded, and chopped
   (about 2 medium)
2 L (8 c) chicken stock
720 ml (3 c) sliced Belgian endive
   (about 3 large)
60 ml (1/4 c) finely chopped garlic
   dill pickle

60 ml (1/4 c) grated Parmesan
cheese
30 ml (2 tbsp) grated Romano cheese
Salt to taste
White pepper to taste

In a large soup pot, melt butter over medium-high heat until it turns a light nutty brown color.

Add leek, onion, red pepper, green pepper, mushrooms, celery, and garlic; sweat stirring occasionally, for 3 to 4 minutes, or until vegetables have wilted slightly.

Stir in tarragon, thyme, oregano, fennel seeds, and sherry.

Add tomatoes and stock, and bring to a boil.

Add endive, reduce heat to medium-low and simmer for 5 minutes.

Stir in pickle and whisk in Parmesan and Romano cheeses.

Cream of Onion and Stilton Cheese
Serves 6 – 8

60 ml (1/4 c) unsalted butter
1 L (4 c) diced onions
(about 2 onions)
60 ml (1/4 c) celery
60 ml (1/4 c) green pepper
2 ml (1/2 tsp) minced garlic
120 ml (1/2 c) white wine
5 ml (1 tsp) Dijon mustard

1 1/2 L (6 c) chicken stock
90 ml (6 tbsp) beurre-manié
345 g (3/4 lb) Stilton cheese, grated
or crumbled
240 ml (1 c) 35% cream
Dash Worcestershire sauce
1 ml (1/4 tsp) ground nutmeg
Salt to taste
White pepper to taste

In a medium-sized, heavy soup pot, melt butter over medium-high heat until it is a nutty brown color.

Add onions, celery, green pepper, and garlic, and sauté for 3 or 4 minutes, stirring occasionally until vegetables are limp.

Add wine, bring to a boil, and reduce by half.

Stir in mustard and chicken stock, bring to a boil, reduce heat to medium, and simmer for 4 or 5 minutes.

In a medium-sized bowl, whisk beurre-manié until smooth.

Slowly whisk in 240 ml (1 c) to 480 ml (2 c) of the soup mixture until beurre-manié resembles a smooth paste.

Whisk into the soup mixture 1 spoonful at a time. Simmer gently to thicken slightly.

Add a small handful of cheese at a time, whisking constantly until melted.

Stir in cream and season with Worcestershire sauce, nutmeg, salt, and pepper and serve.

Chicken Basmati
Serves 6 – 8

60 ml (1/4 c) unsalted butter
2 90-g (3-oz) boned, skinned chicken
   breasts, diced into
   1 cm (1/2 in) cubes
240 ml (1 c) diced Spanish onions
60 ml (1/4 c) diced leek
60 ml (1/4 c) diced green pepper
60 ml (1/4 c) diced celery
80 ml (1/3 c) Basmati rice
5 ml (1 tsp) minced garlic
2 ml (1/2 tsp) dried oregano
2 tomatoes diced
2 L (8 c) chicken stock
Salt to taste
White pepper to taste

In a large, heavy soup pot, melt butter over medium-high heat until foamy.

Add chicken, onion, leek, green pepper, and celery, and sauté, stirring frequently, for 5 minutes, or until chicken turns opaque and vegetables wilt slightly.

Add rice, garlic, oregano, and tomatoes, and continue to sauté for 2 minutes, stirring constantly.

Stir in stock, bring to a boil, reduce heat to medium-low, and simmer for 12 to 15 minutes, or until rice is completely cooked.

Season with salt and pepper to taste and serve.

Cooked, Chilled Gazpacho
Serves 8 – 10

60 ml (1/4 c) unsalted butter
480 ml (2 c) diced Spanish onion
240 ml (1 c) diced carrots
480 ml (2 c) diced celery
480 ml (2 c) diced green pepper
480 ml (2 c) sliced mushrooms
30 ml (2 tbsp) minced garlic
2 ml (1/2 tsp) dried basil
5 ml (1 tsp) dried oregano
30 Italian-type plum tomatoes,
   peeled, seeded and diced
45 ml (3 tbsp) granulated sugar
80 ml (1/3 c) red wine vinegar
2 ml (1/2 tsp) hot pepper sauce
   (optional)
30 ml (2 tbsp) Worcestershire sauce

In a large soup pot, melt butter over medium-high heat.

Add onion, carrots, celery, green pepper, and mushrooms; sweat 3 to 4 minutes, stirring occasionally or until the vegetables have wilted slightly.

Add garlic, basil, and oregano, and continue to cook another 30 seconds.

Add tomatoes, sugar and vinegar.

Bring to a boil, then reduce heat to low and simmer for 40 minutes.

Chill for 12 hours.

Season with pepper sauce, Worcestershire sauce, salt and pepper to taste.

Scampi Stephanie
Serves 2 – 3

60 ml (1/4 c) unsalted butter
120 ml (1/2 c) finely diced leek
120 ml (1/2 c) finely diced onion
2 ml (1/2 tsp) minced garlic
   (1 small clove)
5 ml (1 tsp) finely chopped dill
6 large scampi, with the skin on
5 ml (1 tsp) Armagnac
5 ml (1 tsp) dry sherry
5 ml (1 tsp) Pernod (optional)
1 L (4 c) chicken stock
240 ml (1 c) sliced strawberries
Salt and white pepper to taste

In a medium-sized soup pot, heat butter over medium-high heat until bubbly.

Add leek and onion; sweat for 3 to 4 minutes, stirring occasionally until vegetables are slightly wilted.

Add garlic, dill, and scampi, and continue to cook for 2 or 3 minutes.

Stir in Armagnac, sherry, and Pernod, and bring to a boil.

Stir in stock and return to a boil.

Add strawberries, season with salt and pepper, and serve immediately.

Note: Scampi will toughen if cooked too long.

Chervil
Serves 8

60 ml (1/4 c) butter
3 leeks, sliced
115 g (1/4 lb) potatoes, sliced
600 ml (2 1/2 c) chervil or chervil
   and parsley mixed
1 L (4 c) chicken stock
Juice of **1/2** lemon
15 ml (1 tbsp) dill vinegar or
   white wine vinegar
1 egg yolk
60 ml (1/4 c) 35% cream, whipped

Melt butter in your soup pot, add leeks and cook for 4 minutes.

Add potatoes and chervil and cook for another 2 minutes.

Add stock, cover and simmer for 25 minutes.

Purée in a blender until smooth and return to the pot.

Reheat, adding the lemon juice and vinegar.

Beat eggs yolk in a small bowl.

Add **60 to 75 ml (4 to 5 tbsp)** of hot soup into the egg yolk mix, whisking briskly.

Stir this mixture into the hot soup and do not allow it to boil.

Garnish each serving with a spoonful of whipped cream.

Chicken Noodle
Serves 12 – 14

60 ml (1/4 c) unsalted butter
480 ml (2 c) diced onions
480 ml (2 c) diced leeks
240 ml (1 c) diced carrots
360 ml (1 1/2 c) diced celery
120 ml (1/2 c) sliced mushrooms
60 ml (1/4 c) finely diced sweet red
    pepper or pimento
10 ml (2 tsp) minced garlic
90 g (3 oz) fettuccini noodles, in
    2 1/2 cm (1 in) pieces
3 L (12 c) chicken stock
720 ml (3 c) diced chicken
    (about 3 breasts)
5 ml (1 tsp) Worcestershire sauce
30 ml (2 tbsp) finely diced parsley
Salt to taste
White pepper to taste

In a large soup pot, melt butter over medium-high heat until bubbling.

Add onions, leeks, carrots, celery, mushrooms, and red pepper, cooking until vegetables are wilted, about 6 or 7 minutes, while stirring occasionally.

Add garlic and noodles and continue to cook, stirring frequently, for 5 to 6 minutes, or until noodles are slightly sautéed.

Stir in stock and chicken, bring to a boil, reduce heat to medium-low, and simmer for 20 to 25 minutes, or until chicken and noodles are completely cooked.

Season with Worcestershire sauce, parsley, salt, and pepper and serve.

Crabmeat Rarebit with Beer
Serves 14 – 16

2 1/2 L (10 c) 2% or homogenized
    milk
240 ml (1 c) unsalted butter
720 ml (3 c) diced Spanish onion
120 ml (1/2 c) diced pimento or
    sweet red pepper
360 ml (1 1/4 c) hard or all-purpose
    flour
680 g (1 1/2 lbs) snow crabmeat
120 ml (1/2 c) warm, flat beer
2 ml (1/2 tsp) dried tarragon
5 ml (1 tsp) dried mustard
5 ml (1 tsp) Worcestershire sauce
680 g (1 1/2 lbs) grated aged
    cheddar cheese
240 ml (1 c) 35% cream
2 ml (1/2 tsp) ground nutmeg
Salt and white pepper to taste

Bring milk just to a boil in a large soup pot over medium-high heat.

Meanwhile, in another large, heavy soup pot, melt butter over medium-high heat.

Add onion and pimento and cook until they are wilted, about 3 minutes.

Whisk in flour and continue to cook another 2 to 3 minutes, whisking constantly so as not to brown.

Slowly whisk in **120 ml (1/2 c)** of milk at a time until mixture is smooth.

Simmer until thickened slightly.

Stir in crabmeat, beer, tarragon, mustard, and Worcestershire sauce.

While whisking constantly, add a handful of cheese at a time until cheese has completely melted.

Stir in cream and season with nutmeg, salt, and pepper while returning to the boil before serving.

Scallop Mornay
Serves 8 – 10

60 ml (1/4 c) unsalted butter
240 ml (1 c) finely diced Spanish
  onion
230 g (1/2 lb) scallop pieces
5 ml (1 tsp) minced garlic
60 ml (1/4 c) diced pimento or
  sweet red pepper
5 ml (1 tsp) dried tarragon
120 ml (1/2 c) dry white wine
60 ml (1/4 c) cognac
1 3/4 L (7 c) chicken stock
75 ml (5 tbsp) beurre-manié
230 g (1/2 lb) grated Swiss or
  Gruyère cheese

240 ml (1 c) 35% cream
2 ml (1/2 tsp) ground nutmeg
5 ml (1 tsp) dry mustard
Salt to taste
White pepper to taste

In a large, heavy soup pot, melt butter over medium-high heat.

Add onion, scallops, and garlic, and sauté until onion is translucent but not browned.

Add pimento and tarragon and continue to cook for 3 minutes or until pimento has softened.

Stir in wine, cognac, and chicken stock.

Bring to a boil, then reduce heat to medium and simmer for 5 to 10 minutes.

In a medium-sized bowl, whisk buerre-manié until smooth. Slowly whisk in **240 ml (1 c)** of the soup mixture until beurre-manié resembles a smooth paste.

Add to the soup 1 spoonful at a time, stirring constantly. Simmer gently to thicken slightly.

Add cheese to the soup a handful at a time, stirring constantly until melted.

Stir in cream and season with nutmeg, mustard, salt and pepper.

Serve steaming hot.

Scandinavian Potato

Serves 8 – 10

60 ml (1/4 c) unsalted butter
115 g (4 oz) double-smoked pork,
cut into 1/2 cm (1/4 in) cubes
240 ml (1 c) diced leek
240 ml (1 c) diced onion
1 ml (1/4 tsp) minced garlic
1 ml (1/4 tsp) dried rosemary
480 ml (2 c) peeled, grated potato
(about 3 medium)
2 L (8 c) chicken stock
45 ml (3 tbsp) beurre-manié
120 ml (1/2 c) 35% cream
2 ml (1/2 tsp) Worcestershire sauce
Ground nutmeg to taste
Salt to taste
White pepper to taste

In a medium-sized, heavy soup pot, melt butter over medium-high heat until it turns a nutty brown color.

Add pork and sauté for 1 or 2 minutes, then add leek, onion, garlic, and rosemary and continue to sauté until onion is translucent.

Add potato and cook for 2 to 3 minutes, stirring frequently so as not to burn.

Stir in stock, bring to a boil, reduce heat to medium, and simmer for 20 minutes.

In a medium-sized bowl, whisk beurre-manié until smooth.

Slowly whisk in **240 ml (1 c)** to **480 ml (2 c)** of the soup mixture into the beurre-manié until it resembles a smooth paste, then whisk into the soup 1 spoonful at a time. Simmer gently to thicken slightly.

Stir in cream and season with Worcestershire sauce, nutmeg, salt, and pepper to serve.

Beef Soup Bourgignon

Serves 18

120 ml (1/2 c) olive oil
1 1/2 kg (3 lbs) inside round or sirloin
steak cut into 1 cm (1/2 in) cubes
240 ml (1 c) double-smoked bacon,
cut into 1/2 cm (1/4 in) pieces
30 whole button mushrooms (or
larger mushrooms cut in quarters)
30 pearl onions
120 ml (1/2 c) diced leeks
120 ml (1/2 c) diced carrots
30 ml (2 tbsp) freshly chopped garlic
30 ml (2 tbsp) very finely diced
green peppers
2 bay leaves
15 ml (1 tbsp) chopped fresh tarragon
30 ml (2 tbsp) fresh chopped thyme
90 g (3 oz) good tomato paste
240 ml (1 c) burgundy wine
30 ml (2 tbsp) steak sauce
4 L (16 c) beef stock
360 ml (1 1/2 c) dark roux
Pour oil into a heavy soup pot

on high temperature.

When oil begins to smoke, add beef and stir for 2 to 3 minutes on high heat.

Add bacon, mushrooms and onions while still on high heat and continue stirring for another 3 to 4 minutes.

Add leeks, carrots, garlic, peppers, herbs, tomato paste, wine, steak sauce and beef stock.

Bring to the boil, cover, reduce heat and simmer uncovered for 10 minutes.

Return to the boil, whisk in roux, and reduce heat to a simmer for 3 to 4 minutes before serving.

Fiddlehead
Serves 8

480 ml (2 c) fresh fiddleheads
120 ml (1/2 c) diced leek – white only
120 ml (1/2 c) roasted red peppers, diced
5 ml (1 tsp) diced garlic
120 ml (1/2 c) chili sauce
60 ml (1/4 c) cooked wild rice
5 ml (1 tsp) chopped fresh oregano
1 1/2 L (6 c) vegetable or chicken stock

Rinse fiddleheads thoroughly under cold running water and trim any brown discoloration from stem tips.

Place all ingredients in your soup pot on high heat and bring to the boil.

Boil slowly for 10 minutes, uncovered.

Prosciutto Carmen
Serves 8

230 g (1/2 lb) butter
60 ml (1/4 c) chopped shallots
60 ml (1/4 c) roasted sweet red pepper, finely diced
5 ml (1 tsp) fresh chopped oregano
1 L (4 c) 35% cream
115 g (1/4 lb) ripe Provolone, shredded
460 g (1 lb) prosciutto, sliced julienne
30 ultra-thin slices of raw Spanish onion for garnish

Melt the butter in your soup pot on medium-high, adding shallots, and sauté, while stirring, for 4 to 5 minutes.

Add pepper, oregano and cream while bringing slowly to the boil.

Whisk in cheese until completely melted.

Return to the boil, turn off heat and stir in the prosciutto.

Let stand for 2 minutes, garnish with onion slices and serve.

Purée of Vegetable
Serves 8

2 L (8 c) vegetable stock
120 ml (1/2 c) diced onion
120 ml (1/2 c) diced leek
60 ml (1/4 c) diced carrots
60 ml (1/4 c) diced turnip
60 ml (1/4 c) diced celery root
60 ml (1/4 c) diced celery
60 ml (1/4 c) chopped elephant garlic
230 g (1/2 lb) diced spinach
1 diced red pepper
240 ml (1 c) chili sauce
5 ml (1 tsp) fresh chopped savory

Put all ingredients into your soup pot on high heat and bring to the boil.

Reduce heat and simmer uncovered for 25 minutes.

Remove from stove and purée in blender. (Add soup to blender **480 ml (1 c)** at a time to avoid splashing.)

One Step Pork Stew
Serves 8

2 L (8 c) pork or chicken stock
460 g (1 lb) lean pork, diced into
    1/2 cm (1/2 in) cubes
120 ml (1/2 c) diced onions
60 ml (1/4 c) diced carrots

60 ml (1/4 c) diced turnip
60 ml (1/4 c) diced parsnip
5 ml (1 tsp) chopped garlic
30 ml (2 tbsp) raw pearl barley
120 ml (1/2 c) chili sauce

Put all ingredients into your soup pot on high heat.

Bring to the boil.

Reduce heat and simmer covered for 45 to 50 minutes.

Crazy Pepper
Serves 4

120 ml (1/2 c) puréed, fresh roasted
    jalapenos
1 fresh Scotch bonnet pepper,
    chopped
240 ml (1 c) puréed, fresh roasted
    bell pepper
1 L (4 c) 18% cream
60 ml (1/4 c) fresh chopped
    coriander
5 ml (1 tsp) roasted garlic, chopped

Put all ingredients into a large mixing bowl and whisk thoroughly.

Let stand in fridge for 4 hours.

Whisk again before serving.

Atlantic Salmon with Raspberries
Serves 8

1 L (4 c) fish stock
1 L (4 c) fresh raspberries
460 g (1 lb) Atlantic salmon fillet,
   cut into 1/2 cm (1/4 in) pieces
120 ml (1/2 c) finely diced (sweet)
   onions
120 ml (1/2 c) diced leek
   (use the green closest to the
   white part of the stalk)
30 ml (2 tbsp) fresh chopped dill

Put all ingredients into your soup pot on high heat.

Stir gently while bringing quickly to the boil.

Reduce heat and simmer uncovered for 8 to 10 minutes.

Mexican Cucumber
Serves 8

1 large English cucumber, peeled
   and puréed – approx. 720 ml (3 c)
1 fresh roasted jalapeno pepper,
   also puréed
480 ml (2 c) sour cream
240 ml (1 c) tomato concassée
30 ml (2 tbsp) chopped fresh
   coriander
Juice of 1 large lemon

60 ml (2 oz) Tequila
480 ml (2 c) 18% cream

Put all ingredients into a large mixing bowl and whisk briskly.

Place, covered, in fridge for approximately 4 hours.

Whisk again before serving.

MMMMM Mushrooms!
Serves 8

60 ml (1/4 c) butter
1 L (4 c) sliced button mushrooms
60 g (2 oz) dried porcini mushrooms
60 ml (1/4 c) diced shallots
5 ml (1 tsp) diced garlic
5 ml (1 tsp) chopped fresh tarragon
720 ml (3 c) 35% cream
60 ml (1/4 c) grated Romano cheese

Melt butter in heavy soup pot on high heat before adding all mushrooms and shallots.

Cook 6 to 8 minutes while stirring (until mushrooms are tender).

Add garlic and cook approximately another 2 minutes while continuing to stir.

Add tarragon and cream.

Bring slowly to the boil before reducing heat and simmering 4 to 5 minutes.

Whisk in cheese until melted.

Lamb Stew Tonight
Serves 8 – 10

900 g (2 lbs) lamb diced into
1 cm (1/2 in) pieces

Put lamb in a mixing bowl
with **30 ml (2 tbsp)** diced garlic,
5 ml (1 tsp) chopped rosemary,
15 ml (1 tbsp) chopped thyme
and mix together well.

Preheat oven to 200° C (400° F).

Place meat mixture on a baking
sheet and bake for 20 minutes
or until golden brown.

Remove from oven and pour
240 ml (1 c) of red wine over
the meat mixture (while on the
baking sheet).

Using a spatula, scrape pan for
the renderings.

Soup

240 ml (1 c) diced onion
120 ml (1/2 c) diced carrots
120 ml (1/2 c) diced green pepper
60 ml (1/4 c) chili sauce
60 ml (1/4 c) tomato paste
90 g (3 oz) dried, sliced morel
  mushrooms
230 g (1/2 lb) double-smoked bacon
  – 1/2 cm (1/4 in) cut
2 1/2 L (10 c) lamb or beef stock
60 ml (1/4 c) dark roux

Put all ingredients except roux
into a large soup pot – including
lamb and renderings – and put
on stove on high heat.

Bring to the boil – reduce
heat and simmer covered for
40 minutes.

Bring back to the boil.

Stir a small amount of hot soup
into the roux while mixing well
to a smooth paste – should yield
approximately **240 ml (1 c)**.

Add the roux into the boiling
soup while whisking briskly.

Boil for 2 minutes to cook out flour.

Cherry
Serves 6 – 8

460 g (1 lb) fresh sour cherries
60 ml (1/4 c) sugar
1 L (4 c) water
1 cinnamon stick – 7 1/2 cm (3 in)
  long
2 strips of lemon rind
1 ml (1/4 tsp) salt
30 ml (2 tbsp) "whitewash"
  (equal parts cornstarch and water)
120 ml (1/2 c) dry red wine
60 ml (1/4 c) sour cream

Wash cherries well.

Remove stems and pit the
cherries.

Place in your soup pot sugar,
1 L (4 c) water, cinnamon, lemon
rind and salt.

Bring to the boil over medium heat.

Cover, reduce heat to low and cook 10 minutes.

Remove cinnamon stick and lemon rind.

Add the "whitewash" mixture slowly to soup and mix well, stirring until slightly thickened.

Remove from heat and stir in wine.

Put sour cream in a small bowl, add **240 ml (1 c)** hot soup, and mix well.

Pour mixture into soup pot and mix thoroughly.

Put in covered container and chill.

Serve soup in chilled bowls.

Garnish with sour cream.

Green Onion and Lime

Serves 8 – 10

60 ml (1/4 c) unsalted butter
240 ml (1 c) finely diced leek
(about **1** large)
120 ml (1/2 c) finely diced celery
(**2** medium stalks)
1 1/4 L (5 c) sliced green onions
(about **30**)
5 ml (1 tsp) granulated sugar
2 ml (1/2 tsp) dried tarragon

1 3/4 L (7 c) chicken stock
60 ml (4 tbsp) beurre-manié
120 ml (1/2 c) 35% cream
80 ml (1/3 c) lime juice
(juice of **3** limes)
5 ml (1 tsp) dry mustard
2 ml (1/2 tsp) ground nutmeg
Salt and white pepper to taste

In a large, heavy soup pot, melt butter over medium-high heat or until butter begins to foam slightly.

Add leek and celery; sweat until tender, about 3 or 4 minutes.

Add green onions, sugar, and tarragon, and sauté 5 minutes or until green onions wilt.

Stir in stock and bring to a boil, reduce heat, and simmer 5 to 10 minutes.

In a medium-sized bowl, whisk beurre-manié until smooth.

Slowly whisk in **240 ml (1 c)** of the soup mixture until beurre-manié resembles a smooth paste.

Add to the soup 1 spoonful at a time, whisking constantly.

Simmer until thickened slightly.

Stir in cream and lime juice and season with mustard, nutmeg, salt and pepper.

Simmer for 5 minutes.

Buttermilk and Dill
Serves 8

60 ml (1/4 c) butter
4 leeks, sliced
480 ml (2 c) potatoes, thickly sliced
720 ml (3 c) chicken stock
600 ml (2 1/2 c) buttermilk
90 ml (6 tbsp) chopped dill

Heat butter in soup pot, add leeks and cook gently for 8 minutes.

Add potatoes and then add the stock.

Cover and simmer for 25 to 30 minutes.

Cool slightly, then purée approximately **120 ml (1/2 c)** at a time in blender, with the buttermilk.

Chill in fridge for 8 hours.

Stir in chopped dill shortly before serving.

Celery Consomme with Lovage
Serves 8

1 large bunch of celery, chopped roughly, root, leaves and all
1 1/4 L (5 c) beef stock
Lemon juice to taste
30 ml (2 tbsp) chopped lovage

Put celery and the stock in your soup pot and bring to the boil, very slowly.

Cover and simmer for 30 minutes.

Strain the stock and return it to your soup pot. Discard celery.

Reheat, adding lemon juice.

Stir in the chopped lovage and let stand for 3 or 4 minutes before serving.

Lentil and Herb
Serves 8

1 1/4 L (5 c) veal or chicken stock
120 ml (1/2 c) lentils (red or brown)
25 ml (1 1/2 tbsp) olive oil
1 small onion, chopped
1 clove garlic finely minced
115 g (1/4 lb) spinach, chopped
600 ml (2 1/2 c) chopped mixed herbs
    (sorrel, parsley, chervil, tarragon,
    lovage and lemon thyme)
Juice of **1/2** lemon
160 ml (2/3 c) buttermilk or
    unflavored yogurt

Put stock and lentils in your soup pot on high heat and bring to the boil.

Turn heat down and simmer until lentils are soft.

Heat the oil in a frying pan and sauté the onion until soft and golden, adding garlic halfway through.

Add spinach to the lentils when they are soft.

Simmer until the spinach is cooked, about 8 minutes.

Add the onion and garlic, and the roughly chopped herbs.

Simmer for 2 to 3 minutes.

Cool slightly and purée in a blender.

Heat before serving while adding lemon juice, the buttermilk or yogurt.

Carrot and Turnip Soup with Coriander
Serves 6

45 ml (3 tbsp) butter
230 g (1/2 lb) carrots, cleaned and sliced
230 g (1/2 lb) turnip, sliced
1 L (4 c) chicken stock
30 ml (2 tbsp) sour cream
10 ml (2 tsp) ground coriander
5 ml (1 tsp) ground cumin
15 ml (1 tbsp) finely chopped coriander

Melt butter in your soup pot on medium heat.

Add carrots and turnip and cook for approximately 6 minutes, stirring occasionally.

Add stock and bring to the boil.

Simmer 30 minutes, covered.

Put through a coarse food mill and return to the pot.

Reheat while stirring in sour cream.

Add spices and chopped coriander leaves.

Mix well and let stand for 5 minutes before serving.

Cauliflower with Chervil
Serves 8

60 ml (1/4 c) butter
1 medium cauliflower, cut into florets and then chopped
1 L (4 c) chicken stock
60 ml (1/4 c) 35% cream
45 ml (3 tbsp) chopped chervil

Melt butter in a heavy soup pot.

Add cauliflower and cook for 4 minutes.

Add stock and bring to the boil.

Simmer covered for 20 minutes.

Purée in a blender until smooth and return to your soup pot and reheat.

Stir in the cream.

Chill soup and stir in chervil before serving.

Sorrel and Lettuce
Serves 6

60 ml (1/4 c) butter
240 ml (1 c) sorrel, coarsely chopped
240 ml (1 c) lettuce, coarsely chopped
360 ml (1 1/2 c) parsley, coarsely chopped
120 ml (1/2 c) potato, sliced
600 ml (2 1/2 c) chicken stock
60 ml (1/4 c) 35% cream

Melt butter in a heavy soup pot, add the three green vegetables and simmer for 6 minutes.

Add potato and the chicken stock.

Simmer covered for 25 minutes.

Process through a food mill or coarse sieve.

Return to the pan and reheat.

Stir in cream before serving.

Provençal with Pesto
Serves 12

90 ml (6 tbsp) olive oil
240 ml (1 c) chopped onion
2 small leeks, chopped
2 L (8 c) hot water
240 ml (1 c) carrots, chopped
160 ml (2/3 c) navy beans
240 ml (1 c) zucchini, sliced
360 ml (1 1/2 c) diced snap beans
240 ml (1 c) skinned, chopped tomatoes
120 ml (1/2 c) short macaroni

Soup

Heat oil in a heavy soup pot.

Add onion and leeks and sauté until soft and golden.

Add water, carrots and navy beans and bring to the boil.

Reduce heat and simmer for 45 minutes.

Add zucchini, snap beans and tomatoes and let simmer another 25 minutes.

Add macaroni and cook for approximately 8 minutes more, or until tender.

Pesto

3 cloves garlic finely diced
240 ml (1 c) finely chopped basil leaves
120 ml (1/2 c) fresh grated Parmesan cheese
60 ml (1/4 c) olive oil

Pound garlic to a pulp in a mortar.

Add basil leaves to the garlic, pounding again until the garlic and basil are well blended.

Add grated cheese and continue pounding to a smooth mixture.

Add olive oil to the mix – a drop at a time.

When all is blended, put pesto into a warm tureen and pour the boiling soup over it.

Cover and let stand for 5 minutes.

Bean with Parsley
Serves 8

240 ml (1 c) navy beans
60 ml (1/4 c) olive oil
1 onion, chopped
2 carrots, chopped
2 leeks, chopped
2 stalks celery, chopped
230 g (1/2 lb) tomatoes skinned
   and chopped
60 ml (1/4 c) chicken stock
Sea salt and black pepper (to taste)
90 ml (6 tbsp) chopped parsley

Soak the beans in water for 3 to 4 hours before cooking.

Cook beans until tender, approximately 45 minutes.

Drain, reserving the water.

Heat oil in your soup pot on high heat and cook the onion until slightly softened.

Add carrots, leeks, and celery and cook for another 5 to 6 minutes.

Add tomatoes and cook for a further 3 to 4 minutes.

Heat the stock and pour it into the soup pot. (If you do not have enough stock, use some of the liquid from the beans.)

Bring to the boil, reduce heat and simmer 30 minutes, until the vegetables are soft.

Add beans and reheat.

Season with sea salt and black pepper to taste.

Stir in chopped parsley before serving.

Chilled Chinese B.B.Q. Duck with Black Cherries
Serves 12

460 g (1 lb) B.B.Q. duck de-boned,
   skinned, and chopped in
   1/2 cm (1/4 in) pieces
120 ml (1/2 c) black cherry jam
4 cans black cherries in syrup
5 ml (1 tsp) dried fresh ginger
480 ml (2 c) sour cream
1 L (4 c) 18% cream
60 ml (2 oz) black cherry liqueur
15 ml (1 tbsp) zest of orange
15 ml (1 tbsp) zest of lemon
90 ml (3 oz) Hoisin sauce

Mix all ingredients in a bowl, whisking briskly.

Then let stand in the fridge for 8 hours.

Whisk again before serving.

Matzo Ball
Serves 10

240 ml (1 c) diced onion
240 ml (1 c) diced celery
5 ml (1 tsp) diced garlic
2 L (8 c) chicken stock
120 ml (1/2 c) finely diced carrots
20 matzo balls

Put all ingredients except matzo balls into your soup pot and bring to the boil.

Add matzo balls and boil for 8 to 10 minutes.

Remove from heat and serve.

Tarragon
Serves 6

6 sprigs tarragon
1 L (4 c) strong chicken stock
30 ml (2 tbsp) butter
15 ml (1 tbsp) flour
1 egg yolk
60 ml (1/4 c) 35% cream
25 ml (1 1/2 tbsp) lemon juice

Select the best leaves from the tarragon sprigs and save for garnish.

Pour stock into your soup pot, adding the remaining tarragon (sprigs and all) and bring to the boil.

Cover, remove from heat and let stand for 20 minutes.

Melt butter in another soup pot, add flour and stir well until blended.

Add stock to this, poured through a sieve, and simmer for 3 to 4 minutes stirring constantly.

Beat egg yolk in a bowl with the cream and stir in a few spoonfuls of the hot soup.

Add the egg yolk mixture and lemon juice to the soup.

Chop the reserved tarragon leaves and scatter on the top of each serving.

Jellied Cucumber and Mint
Serves 6

1 L (4 c) chicken stock
1 shallot, peeled and chopped
1 cucumber (remove about half
    the skin and grate coarsely)
30 ml (2 tbsp) lemon juice
1 envelope gelatin
45 ml (3 tbsp) chopped mint
Lemon quarters

Heat chicken stock in your soup pot, add shallots and cook for 4 minutes.

Add the grated cucumber and lemon juice while stirring.

Dissolve gelatin in a little of the stock and add this mixture to the soup pot.

Leave to cool.

When half set, stir in the mint, and chill once more.

Serve with lemon quarters.

Clam
Serves 6

24 cherrystone clams
45 ml (3 tbsp) olive oil
2 cloves of garlic, peeled and minced
1 L (4 c) peeled ripe tomatoes,
   coarsely chopped
60 ml (1/4 c) white wine
60 ml (4 tbsp) chopped Italian
   flat-leaf parsley

Scrub clams and soak for 30 minutes, covered in cold water.

Heat oil in a large soup pot, add garlic and sauté for 1 minute.

Add tomatoes and wine and bring to the boil.

Reduce heat to low and simmer for 15 minutes; keep warm.

In a large frying pan with close-fitting lid, bring **240 ml (1 c)** water to the boil.

Drain the clams well and add to the pan.

Cover, steam 5 to 10 minutes, until clams open.

Place an equal number of clams in each soup bowl, reserving the broth.

Strain broth through cheesecloth to remove any sand or grit and add clam broth to the tomato mixture.

Mix well before pouring over the open clams in each bowl.

Sprinkle each serving with parsley.

Lemon Curry Chicken
Serves 8

90 ml (6 tbsp) raw rice
2 L (8 c) chicken stock
4 eggs
60 ml (4 tbsp) lemon juice
2 ml (1/2 tsp) curry powder
15 ml (1 tbsp) parsley

In a heavy soup pot, bring rice and stock to a boil.

Reduce heat and simmer for 20 minutes, or until rice is tender.

In a bowl, beat the eggs, lemon juice and curry powder.

When well blended, mix in **45 ml (3 tbsp)** of stock.

Add the egg mixture slowly to the simmering soup and stir for another 5 minutes.

Sprinkle with parsley before serving.

Tandoori Vegetable
Serves 10

30 g (1 oz) chopped garlic
240 ml (1 c) diced onion
240 ml (1 c) diced green pepper
120 ml (1/2 c) diced celery
120 ml (1/2 c) diced carrots
120 ml (1/2 c) diced parsnips
120 ml (1/2 c) diced fennel
240 ml (1 c) peeled, seeded
   tomatoes, chopped
5 ml (1 tsp) julienne ginger
60 ml (1/4 c) red lentils
60 ml (1/4 c) tandoori powder
2 1/2 L (10 c) vegetable stock
30 ml (1 oz) lemon juice

Bring all ingredients to a boil in a large soup pot, on high heat.

Turn heat down and simmer, covered, for 40 minutes.

Chilled Apricot
Serves 2

1 can of apricot halves
240 ml (1 c) sour cream

Chill apricot halves and drain.

Blend apricots in a blender.

Add sour cream and continue to blend until well mixed.

Chill in fridge 6 to 8 hours.

Buffalo Bisque
Serves 14

900 g (2 lbs) boned buffalo meat,
   cut into **1 cm (1/2 in)** pieces
230 g (1/2 lb) double-smoked bacon,
   cut into **1 cm (1/2 in)** pieces
30 ml (2 tbsp) minced garlic
240 ml (1 c) diced onion
240 ml (1 c) diced carrots
120 ml (1/2 c) diced green pepper
120 ml (1/2 c) diced celery
120 ml (1/2 c) dry red wine
2 1/2 L (10 c) buffalo or beef stock
120 ml (1/2 c) Port wine
120 ml (4 oz) black currant jelly
120 ml (1/2 c) chili sauce
115 g (4 oz) dried porcini mushrooms
120 ml (1/2 c) dark roux

Preheat oven to 190° C (375° F).

On a baking sheet mix buffalo meat, smoked bacon, garlic, onion, carrots, green pepper, celery, and spread evenly.

Bake for 40 minutes.

Remove baked ingredients from oven.

Pour red wine over the baking sheet and scrape up the renderings with a wooden spoon.

Pour baked items and renderings into a large soup pot, adding stock, Port, jelly, chili sauce and porcini mushrooms.

Turn on high heat and bring to the boil for 30 minutes.

In a steel mixing bowl whisk **240 ml (1 c)** of the boiling soup with the roux.

Then transfer the roux mixture into the boiling soup while stirring.

When the soup begins to thicken, return to the boil for 3 minutes to cook out the flour.

Remove from heat and serve.

Garden Greens with Cheddar
Serves 8

1 1/2 L (6 c) chicken velouté
460 g (1 lb) mixed garden greens (called California greens in some supermarkets)
240 ml (1 c) diced onions
240 ml (1 c) diced mushrooms
15 ml (1 tbsp) chopped garlic
60 ml (1/4 c) chopped basil
240 ml (1 c) dry white wine
460 g (1 lb) spinach, cleaned and stemmed
240 ml (1 c) shredded medium cheddar cheese
60 ml (1/4 c) grated Parmesan cheese

In an over-sized soup pot placed on high heat, bring the chicken velouté, and the next seven ingredients to a boil and cook for 5 to 7 minutes.

Whisk in the cheeses and keep whisking until completely melted.

Garlic
Serves 4

80 ml (1/3 c) olive oil
60 ml (1/4 c) butter
8 cloves of garlic, peeled
2 ml (1/2 tsp) paprika
Dash of cayenne
720 ml (3 c) bread cubes (croutons)
1 1/2 L (6 c) boiling water

Pour oil into a heavy soup pot, add butter and heat until butter is melted.

Add garlic and sauté until golden brown.

Remove garlic, mash well, and set aside.

Add spices to soup pot and toss in bread cubes.

Sauté bread cubes until golden brown, then remove and set aside on absorbent paper to dry.

Add the water to the soup pot, reserving a little water to blend the garlic into a paste.

Add the garlic paste into the soup and bring to the boil.

Reduce heat and simmer uncovered for 30 minutes.

Garnish with bread cubes for serving.

Beef Mushroom

Serves 8

60 ml (1/4 c) oil
900 g (2 lbs) sirloin steak,
    cut into **1 cm (1/2 in)** pieces
480 ml (2 c) sliced button
    mushrooms
115 g (4 oz) brown cep mushrooms
240 ml (1 c) sliced shiitake
    mushrooms
115 g (1/4 lb) diced double-smoked
    bacon
240 ml (1 c) diced onion
60 ml (1/4 c) diced green pepper
60 ml (1/4 c) wild rice
60 ml (1/4 c) Port wine
60 ml (1/4 c) tomato paste
2 L (8 c) beef stock

Heat oil in your soup pot on high heat.

When the oil begins to smoke, add beef and cook for 8 minutes while stirring.

Add mushrooms, bacon, onion, green pepper and cook for 5 minutes.

Add rice, Port, tomato paste and beef stock.

Bring to the boil, reduce heat and simmer for 40 minutes.

Spiced Lentil and Chorizo

Serves 6

30 ml (2 tbsp) virgin olive oil
285 g (10 oz) uncooked chorizo
    sausage, sliced on the diagonal
    into **1 cm (1/2 in)** pieces
2 cloves garlic roughly chopped
1 fresh or dried red chili, seeds
    removed, roughly chopped
1 onion finely chopped
1 large red bell pepper, cored,
    seeded and finely chopped
230 g (1/2 lb) red lentils
1 1/4 L (5 c) chicken stock

Heat the oil in your soup pot and add the chorizo, sautéing over moderately high heat while stirring until the chorizo is well browned.

Once cooked, reserve the chorizo, after removing it from the pot with a slotted spoon.

With a mortar and pestle, pound the garlic and chili to a paste.

Return the pot to the heat and add the paste, onion and 1/2 of the chopped bell pepper.

Cook over low heat for 5 minutes.

Add the lentils and stock and bring to the boil.

Reduce heat, cover and simmer for 15 minutes or until lentils are tender, adding more liquid if soup becomes too thick.

Add the chorizo and remaining bell pepper and return to the boil before serving.

Grandma's Cream of Tomato
Serves 8

120 ml (1/2 c) 35% cream
120 ml (1/2 c) tomato paste
2 L (8 c) peeled, seeded, chopped
   tomatoes
120 ml (1/2 c) diced onion
120 ml (1/2 c) diced green pepper
240 ml (1 c) tomato juice
2 bay leaves
1 whole clove of garlic

Reserve the 35% cream and **120 ml (1/2 c)** tomato paste.

Bring all other ingredients to a boil on high heat.

Turn heat down, and simmer, covered, for 20 minutes.

Remove from heat.

Using a wooden ladle, force the soup through a medium-sized strainer into a bowl.

Pour strained soup back into the pot and set on high heat.

Add tomato paste and the cream and bring to the boil before serving.

Blue Scallop
Serves 12

60 ml (1/4 c) butter
360 ml (1 1/2 c) bay scallops
240 ml (1 c) diced onion
120 ml (1/2 c) diced red pepper
15 ml (1 tbsp) chopped garlic
15 ml (1 tbsp) diced
   sun-dried tomatoes
15 ml (1 tbsp) dried tarragon
30 ml (1 oz) brandy
240 ml (1 c) dry white wine
2 L (8 c) fish velouté
120 ml (1/2 c) 35% cream
240 ml (1 c) shredded Danish
   blue cheese
60 ml (1/4 c) grated Parmesan
   cheese

Melt butter on high heat and add scallops, onion, green pepper, garlic, tomato and tarragon.

Cook on high heat for 6 minutes while stirring.

Add the brandy and the wine and cook to reduce by half.

Add velouté.

Bring the soup to the boil, add cream and whisk in cheeses until completely melted.

Bad Brad's Hot Chili
Serves 8

60 ml (1/4 c) oil
460 g (1 lb) ground beef
240 ml (1 c) diced onion
240 ml (1 c) diced green pepper
60 ml (1/4 c) diced Scotch bonnet
    peppers
60 ml (1/4 c) dried chilies
15 ml (1 tbsp) chopped garlic
120 ml (1/2 c) chili sauce
2 300-ml (10-oz) cans plum
    tomatoes, crushed
5 ml (1 tsp) dried basil
5 ml (1 tsp) dried oregano
2 bay leaves
120 ml (1/2 c) chili powder
60 ml (1/4 c) powdered beef base
1 360-ml (12-oz) can red kidney
    beans

Pour oil into a heavy soup pot.

When oil gets hot add ground beef and cook, stirring all the while until brown.

Add the rest of the ingredients, except the beans, and bring to the boil.

Turn heat down and simmer uncovered for 30 minutes.

Bring back to the boil, add beans and serve.

Spiced Carrot and Orange
Serves 6

45 ml (3 tbsp) canola oil
1 onion, roughly chopped
600 ml (2 1/2 c) carrots, thinly sliced
2 ml (1/2 tsp) ground coriander
1 L (4 c) chicken or vegetable stock
60 ml (1/4 c) orange juice
15 ml (1 tbsp) orange zest julienne
    and 12 crushed coriander seeds
    for garnish

Heat oil in your soup pot and add onion.

Sauté for 5 minutes, until soft.

Add the carrots and coriander, cover and simmer for 5 minutes stirring occasionally.

Add stock and bring to the boil.

Reduce heat, cover and stir occasionally for 30 minutes, or until carrots are tender.

Process in a blender until smooth.

Work through a strainer into a clean pot.

Add orange juice and reheat adding more stock if soup is too thick.

Serve hot with orange and coriander garnish.

Drunken Squash
Serves 10

1 L (4 c) diced, peeled acorn squash
230 g (1/2 lb) butter
240 ml (1 c) diced onion
120 ml (1/2 c) diced red pepper
1/2 of a cinnamon stick
4 whole cloves
120 ml (1/2 c) brown sugar
60 ml (1/4 c) molasses
120 ml (1/2 c) dry sherry
1 1/2 L (6 c) béchamel sauce
240 ml (1 c) brandy
60 ml (1/4 c) 35% cream

Bake squash in the oven at 190° C (375° F) for 20 minutes.

Melt butter on medium-high heat, add squash, onion, red pepper, cinnamon, cloves and cook for 10 minutes while stirring.

Add sugar, molasses and sherry and cook for 2 minutes while stirring.

Add béchamel and return to the boil.

Stir in brandy and cream before serving.

Wild Boar Stew
Serves 12

60 ml (1/4 c) vegetable oil
900 g (2 lbs) loin of boar,
    cut into 1 cm (1/2 in) pieces
240 ml (1 c) double-smoked bacon,
    cubed into 1 cm (1/2 in) pieces
120 ml (1/2 c) dry red wine
120 ml (1/2 c) Port wine
3 L (12 c) pork or beef stock
240 ml (1 c) peeled pearl onions
240 ml (1 c) diced potatoes
120 ml (1/2 c) diced carrots
60 ml (1/4 c) pearl barley
60 ml (1/4 c) diced green pepper
120 ml (1/2 c) sauerkraut
120 ml (1/2 c) tomato paste
180 g (6 oz) dried porcini mushrooms
30 ml (2 tbsp) chopped fresh sage

Heat oil in a heavy soup pot, on high heat.

When oil begins to smoke, add boar meat and cook for 8 to 10 minutes, while stirring.

Add smoked bacon and cook for 5 more minutes.

Add wines and reduce liquid by half.

Add stock and all other ingredients and bring to the boil.

Reduce heat and simmer for 60 to 80 minutes.

Beef Borscht
Serves 8

2 L (8 c) beef stock
230 g (1/2 lb) chuck steak
1 small onion, peeled and studded
    with **1** or **2** cloves
1 carrot sliced
2 celery stalks roughly chopped
460 g (1 lb) fresh beets, cooked in
    advance and cooled
1 bouquet garni
30 ml (2 tbsp) red wine vinegar
30 ml (2 tbsp) tomato paste
5 ml (1 tsp) sugar
Sour cream

Bring to a boil, stock, beef, onion, carrot, celery, beets, and bouquet garni.

Skim, cover and simmer for 1 hour.

Remove the beef and let cool.

Peel the beets and cut into matchsticks.

Cut the beef into matchsticks.

Strain the stock and pour into clean pot.

Add vinegar, tomato paste, and sugar and bring to the boil while stirring.

Add "matchsticked" beef and the beets to the boiling stock and cook 5 to 6 minutes.

Serve hot, garnished with sour cream.

Steak and Kidney
with Red Wine
Serves 10

60 ml (1/4 c) vegetable oil
460 g (1 lb) sirloin steak, raw,
    cut into **1 cm (1/2 in)** pieces
460 g (1 lb) veal kidneys, washed,
    blanched, diced into **1 cm (1/2 in)**
    pieces
240 ml (1 c) sliced mushrooms
240 ml (1 c) diced onion
115 g (4 oz) side bacon, diced
30 ml (2 tbsp) tomato paste
120 ml (1/2 c) dry red wine
2 L (8 c) demi-glace

Heat oil in a heavy soup pot on high.

When oil gets hot, add steak and kidneys and cook until brown.

Add mushrooms, onion, and bacon, and cook, while stirring, for 3 minutes.

Add tomato paste and wine.

Reduce by 1/3.

Add demi-glace and return to the boil.

Sugar Plum
Serves 4

480 ml (2 c) water
240 ml (1 c) fruity white wine
30 ml (2 tbsp) sugar
30 ml (2 tbsp) brandy
1 cinnamon stick
Zest and juice of **1/2** orange
460 g (1 lb) red plums, halved
  and pitted
120 ml (1/2 c) sour cream

Gently heat water, wine and sugar until the sugar is dissolved.

Add the brandy, cinnamon stick and orange zest and bring to the boil.

Turn heat down and simmer for 10 minutes or until syrupy.

Remove and discard the cinnamon stick and orange zest.

Add the plums and return to the boil.

Turn heat down, cover and simmer for 10 minutes or until fruit is soft, stirring occasionally.

Process soup in a blender until smooth, then strain into a bowl.

Let cool, stir in the orange juice and sour cream until evenly mixed.

Chill for 8 hours and serve.

Good ol' Boys' Hog Chowder
Serves 8

120 ml (1/2 c) oil
360 ml (1 1/2 c) diced pork loin –
  1 cm (1/2 in) cubes
60 ml (1/4 c) diced garlic
120 ml (1/2 c) diced onion
120 ml (1/2 c) diced leek
60 ml (1/4 c) chopped jalepeno
  peppers
60 ml (1/4 c) diced green pepper
720 ml (3 c) beef stock
720 ml (3 c) barbecue sauce

Put oil into a heavy soup pot on high heat until oil begins to smoke.

Add pork, browning well on all sides, while stirring, approximately 5 to 6 minutes.

While still on high heat, add garlic and all vegetables and cook, while stirring, until garlic turns a golden brown.

Add beef stock and barbecue sauce.

Reduce heat and simmer, covered, 10 minutes.

Note: Real *"good ol' boys"* tell me that they frequently add hot sauce to taste.

Chilled Sour Cherry
Serves 10

1 L (4 c) pitted, puréed, fresh sour
    cherries
480 ml (2 c) sour cream
240 ml (1 c) ricotta cheese
30 ml (2 tbsp) chopped fresh
    spearmint
240 ml (1 c) cherry brandy
720 ml (3 c) 18% cream
240 ml (1 c) cherry jam or jelly

Place all ingredients into a large
mixing bowl.

Whisk together well.

Refrigerate for approximately
4 hours.

Whisk again before serving.

Cajun Seafood
Serves 8 – 10

240 ml (1 c) peeled raw shrimp
120 ml (1/2 c) raw bay scallops
120 ml (1/2 c) raw abalone, julienned
120 ml (1/2 c) raw conch meat,
    julienned
1 jalapeno pepper, diced fine
15 ml (1 tbsp) diced, fresh garlic
120 ml (1/2 c) diced onion
120 ml (1/2 c) diced green of leek
60 ml (1/4 c) finely diced yam

120 ml (1/2 c) chili sauce
2 L (8 c) tomato juice
480 ml (2 c) fish stock
120 ml (1/2 c) fresh chopped
    coriander
Salt and pepper to taste

Put all ingredients (except
coriander) into a large soup pot
and bring to the boil, covered.

Reduce heat and simmer
20 minutes.

Add coriander. Season to taste.

Return briefly to a boil.

Orange
Serves 4

900 ml (3 3/4 c) water
60 ml (1/4 c) "whitewash"
    (equal parts cornstarch and water)
600 ml (2 1/2 c) orange juice
60 ml (1/4 c) sugar
Whipped cream and thin orange
    slices for garnish

Bring the water to the boil.

Whisk the "whitewash" into the
boiling water to thicken slightly.

Add the orange juice and sugar.

Garnish each bowl with a dollop
of whipped cream and a thin
slice of orange.

This soup can also be
served hot.

Zucchini Flowers with Cheese and Sun-Dried Tomatoes
Serves 6 – 8

60 ml (1/4 c) extra virgin olive oil
720 ml (3 c) washed and chopped
zucchini flowers (remove stems)
120 ml (1/2 c) diced leeks,
white part only
120 ml (1/2 c) roasted, diced red
peppers
15 ml (1 tbsp) chopped garlic
15 ml (1 tbsp) chopped, fresh
oregano
30 ml (2 tbsp) chopped, sun-dried
tomatoes
480 ml (2 c) chicken stock
1 L (4 c) tomato concassée
Salt to taste
115 g (1/4 lb) aged (strong)
Provolone cheese, shredded

Heat olive oil in your soup pot on high heat.

Add zucchini flowers and leek and stir-fry in oil for 5 to 6 minutes.

Add all other ingredients – except cheese – and bring to the boil.

Reduce heat and simmer for 10 minutes.

Bring back to the boil and whisk in cheese.

Continue whisking until cheese is completely melted and blended into the soup.

Bison Tenderloin
Serves 6 – 8

60 ml (1/4 c) butter
240 ml (1 c) diced Spanish onion
80 ml (1/3 c) diced green peppers
80 ml (1/3 c) diced leeks
15 ml (1 tbsp) fresh rosemary
460 g (1 lb) well-browned bison cut
into **1/2 cm (1/4 in)** cubes
1 1/2 L (6 c) beef stock
60 ml (1/4 c) cooked wild rice
60 ml (1/4 c) diced roasted red
peppers
260 g (9 oz) chopped porcini
mushrooms
2 bay leaves
1 large garlic clove, chopped

Heat butter on high heat in your soup pot.

When butter melts add onions, green peppers, leeks, rosemary and bison.

Cook while stirring for 4 to 5 minutes.

Add stock and all other ingredients.

Bring to the boil and continue boiling approximately 10 minutes.

Sour Cherries with Pork
Serves 8

1 L (4 c) pork or chicken stock
1 L (4 c) pitted, fresh sour cherries
  (mashed or puréed)
460 g (1 lb) pork tenderloin, diced
  into 1/2 cm (1/4 in) cubes
60 ml (1/4 c) diced leek greens
120 ml (1/2 c) cherry brandy
60 ml (2 oz) Cassis liqueur
60 ml (1/4 c) cooked wild rice
15 ml (1 tbs) Hoisin sauce

Put all ingredients into your soup pot on high heat and bring to a rolling boil.

Cover, and continue to boil 8 to 10 minutes.

Curried Apple
Serves 10

720 ml (3 c) Spy or Macintosh
  apples, peeled, cored, and diced
  into 1/2 cm (1/4 in) cubes
45 ml (3 tbsp) curry powder
480 ml (2 c) apple juice
480 ml (2 c) sour cream
240 ml (1 c) hard apple cider
60 ml (1/4 c) lemon juice
720 ml (3 c) mango chutney
240 ml (1 c) 35% cream

Put all ingredients into a large mixing bowl and whisk well.

Let stand in fridge for 4 hours.

Whisk again before serving.

Smoked Duck with Swiss Chard
Serves 10

1 1/2 L (6 c) duck or chicken stock
120 ml (1/2 c) diced onion
680 g (1 1/2 lbs) chopped fresh
  Swiss chard (leaves only)
1 large garlic clove, diced
680 g (1 1/2 lbs) deboned, smoked
  duck meat cut into 1/2 cm (1/4 in)
  pieces
2 eggs, well beaten
120 ml (1/2 c) shredded Danish
  blue cheese

Bring stock to a boil in your soup pot.

Add onion, Swiss chard and garlic, boiling another 5 to 6 minutes.

Add duck meat.

Reduce heat as you whisk in eggs and cheese.

Continue stirring until cheese is completely melted.

Old Fashioned Short Ribs

Serves 8 – 10

1 1/4 kg (2 1/2 lbs) short ribs chopped into **1 cm (1/2 in)** pieces
45 ml (3 tbsp) red wine
3 tomatoes, peeled, seeded and chopped
1 medium potato, coarsely chopped
1 parsnip, coarsely chopped
120 ml (1/2 c) chopped carrots
120 ml (1/2 c) zucchini, coarsely chopped
60 ml (1/4 c) squash, coarsely chopped
3 garlic cloves, minced
30 ml (2 tbsp) barley
2 ml (1/2 tsp) fresh thyme, chopped
2 ml (1/2 tsp) fresh tarragon, chopped
2 L (8 c) cold water

Preheat oven to 200° C (400° F), brown the short ribs in a roasting pan.

When fully browned, transfer ribs to a large stewing pot.

Deglaze the roasting pan with wine thoroughly, adding mixture to the stewing pot.

Add all other ingredients to the stewing pot and bring to the boil.

Reduce heat to a simmer and cook, covered, for 1 hour.

Veal with Mustard

Serves 10

60 ml (1/4 c) olive oil
460 g (1 lb) ground veal
15 ml (1 tbsp) diced garlic
240 ml (1 c) diced leeks
45 ml (3 tbsp) Basmati rice
1 1/2 L (6 c) veal or beef stock
120 ml (1/2 c) roasted parsnips (puréed)
60 ml (1/4 c) Dijon mustard
120 ml (1/2 c) sour cream

Add olive oil to your soup pot on high heat.

Still on high heat, add veal and brown well while stirring.

Add garlic, leeks and rice stirring briskly for two minutes.

Add stock, parsnip and mustard and bring to the boil.

Reduce heat to a simmer and cook, covered, for 15 minutes.

Return to a boil while whisking in sour cream.

Buttermilk and Brie with Capers
Serves 6

720 ml (3 c) buttermilk
480 ml (2 c) chicken stock
460 g (1 lb) ripe Brie, cleaned and
   chopped into **1 cm (1/2 in)** pieces
240 ml (1 c) 35% cream
60 ml (1/4 c) capers

Bring buttermilk and stock to the boil in your soup pot.

Reduce heat and simmer for 10 to 12 minutes.

Whisk in Brie until completely melted.

Stir in cream and capers.

Return briefly to the boil before serving.

Tomato and Onion
Serves 8

60 ml (1/4 c) extra virgin olive oil
1 L (4 c) Spanish onion, coarsely
   chopped
60 ml (1/4 c) fresh, diced fennel
120 ml (1/2 c) diced green peppers
45 ml (3 tbsp) chopped garlic
30 ml (2 tbsp) chopped, fresh
   oregano
1 1/2 L (6 c) tomato concassée

Put olive oil into your soup pot on high heat.

When oil begins to smoke, add onions, fennel, and peppers.

Cook 6 to 8 minutes while stirring.

Stir in garlic and oregano while stirring another 2 minutes.

Add tomato concassée and bring to the boil.

Reduce heat to a simmer, cover, and cook for 10 minutes, stirring occasionally.

Return to the boil before serving.

Honeydew
Serves 4 – 6

1 large honeydew melon, peeled,
   pitted and puréed in blender
480 ml (2 c) 18% cream
240 ml (1 c) sour cream
15 ml (1 tbsp) diced fresh mint
60 ml (1/4 c) melon liqueur
30 ml (2 tbsp) white sugar

Place all ingredients into a large mixing bowl and whisk briskly.

Refrigerate for approximately 4 hours.

Whisk again before serving.

Cheese and Eggs in Broth
Serves 8

1 L (4 c) chicken stock
120 ml (1/2 c) shredded medium
    yellow cheddar
120 ml (1/2 c) grated Parmesan
120 ml (1/2 c) shredded Danish blue
    cheese
6 large eggs
15 ml (1 tbsp) chopped fresh parsley
120 ml (1/2 c) 35% cream

Put chicken stock in your soup pot
on high heat and bring to a boil.

Whisk in eggs and return to the
boil.

Add cheese, stirring until
completely melted.

Whisk in parsley and cream.

Return briefly to the boil before
serving.

Spicy Chilled Scampi
Serves 6

720 ml (3 c) cooked scampi chopped
    into 1 cm (1/2 in) pieces
480 ml (2 c) ricotta cheese
120 ml (1/2 c) sour cream
1 small bunch green onions, finely
    diced
1 medium jalapeno pepper,
    finely diced

30 ml (2 tbsp) chopped fresh
    coriander
60 ml (2 oz) Galliano liqueur
5 ml (1 tsp) Spanish paprika
480 ml (2 c) 18% cream

Put all ingredients into a large
mixing bowl and whisk well.

Refrigerate for not less than
4 hours.

Whisk again before serving.

Note: May need **15 ml (1 tbsp)**
salt for taste.

Mexican Bean
Serves 6 – 8

60 ml (1/4 c) tomato juice
1 1/2 L (6 c) canned red kidney
    beans – puréed
120 ml (1/2 c) avocado purée
1 diced jalapeno pepper
60 ml (1/4 c) chopped coriander
480 ml (2 c) buttermilk
15 ml (1 tbsp) julienned lemon zest
120 ml (1/2 c) sour cream

Place all ingredients into your
soup pot at medium-high heat.

Slowly bring to the boil while
whisking.

When soup reaches the boiling
point, turn off heat and let stand
5 minutes before serving.

May require **30 ml (2 tbsp)** salt
for flavoring.

Oysters in Bourbon and Cheese
Serves 4

20 fresh shucked oysters (reserve liquid)
120 ml (1/2 c) bourbon
720 ml (3 c) 35% cream
120 ml (1/2 c) shredded Stilton
120 ml (1/2 c) shredded Gorgonzola

Flambé bourbon on high heat until flame goes out.

Add cream and oyster juice.

Bring to the boil, reduce heat immediately and simmer for 2 minutes.

Whisk in cheeses until completely melted.

Add oysters to simmering soup and cook no more than 2 minutes more.

Crab and Tomato
Serves 6 – 8

60 ml (1/4 c) extra virgin olive oil
120 ml (1/2 c) diced onion
120 ml (1/2 c) diced red peppers
45 ml (3 tbsp) finely chopped garlic
460 g (1 lb) snow crab meat
1 1/2 L (6 c) tomato concassée

120 ml (1/2 c) Riesling wine
2 bay leaves
15 ml (1 tbsp) fresh chopped tarragon

Put oil in your soup pot on high heat.

When oil is hot, add onions and red peppers and cook 5 minutes while stirring constantly.

Add chopped garlic and cook another 2 minutes.

Add all other ingredients.

Bring to the boil, then reduce heat and simmer for approximately 20 minutes.

Mexican Tomato
Serves 6 – 8

60 ml (1/4 c) olive oil
120 ml (1/2 c) diced onion
120 ml (1/2 c) diced green pepper
60 ml (1/4 c) diced Jalapeno pepper (do not remove seeds)
2 diced garlic cloves
60 ml (1/4 c) chopped coriander
15 ml (1 tbsp) chili powder
1/2 of a ripe avocado, puréed
240 ml (1 c) tomato juice
1 L (4 c) fresh tomato sauce

Heat olive oil in your soup pot until it begins to smoke.

Still on high heat, add onion,

peppers and garlic stirring until garlic turns golden brown.

Add coriander and chili powder, then avocado, tomato juice and tomato sauce.

Bring to the boil.

Reduce heat and simmer for 20 minutes, stirring occasionally.

Cauliflower with Stilton
Serves 6

80 ml (1/3 c) clarified butter
240 ml (1 c) chopped red onion
345 g (3/4 lb) chopped cauliflower
1 L (4 c) chicken stock
60 ml (1/4 c) raw orzo pasta
80 ml (1/3 c) 35% cream
120 ml (1/2 c) shredded Stilton

With butter on high heat in your soup pot, add onions and cauliflower and cook 5 to 6 minutes while stirring.

Add stock and pasta and bring to the boil.

Reduce heat and simmer for 7 minutes or until pasta is *al dente*.

Add cream and return to the boil.

Whisk in cheese and return to boil before serving.

Smoked Chicken Florentine
Serves 8

60 ml (1/4 c) clarified butter
680 g (1 1/2 lbs) smoked boneless chicken cut into **1/2 cm (1/4 in)** cubes
120 ml (1/2 c) diced onion
1 garlic clove, minced
60 ml (1/4 c) white wine
2 L (8 c) chicken stock
900 g (2 lbs) spinach, cleaned and chopped
120 ml (1/2 c) fresh chopped basil
2 eggs, beaten lightly
120 ml (1/2 c) grated Parmesan cheese
White pepper to taste

Heat butter in your soup pot on medium-high heat.

Add chicken and garlic, sautéing for 2 to 3 minutes until onion wilts slightly.

Add stock and wine and bring to the boil.

Reduce heat immediately and simmer for 3 minutes.

Add spinach and basil and simmer an additional 4 to 5 minutes, stirring occasionally.

Whisk in beaten eggs and Parmesan before serving and add white pepper if desired.

Sour Mushroom
Serves 6 – 8

60 ml (1/4 c) clarified butter
40 small button mushrooms
60 ml (1/4 c) diced onion
60 ml (1/4 c) diced leek
60 ml (1/4 c) diced red pepper
60 ml (1/4 c) chopped fresh basil
30 ml (2 tbsp) chopped fresh oregano
30 ml (2 tbsp) chopped fresh garlic
30 ml (2 tbsp) uncooked long grain rice
1 1/2 L (6 c) chicken stock
120 ml (1/2 c) lemon juice

Heat butter in your soup pot on high heat.

Add mushrooms, onion, leek and red pepper and cook on high 5 to 6 minutes while stirring.

Add herbs, garlic and rice, and cook 2 minutes more on high heat.

Add chicken stock and bring to the boil.

Reduce to a simmer, cover, and cook 15 minutes.

Add lemon juice.

Return to the boil for approximately 2 minutes before serving.

Watermelon with Lime and Kiwi
Serves 4 – 6

720 ml (3 c) puréed watermelon flesh, seeded
4 kiwi fruit, peeled and julienned
240 ml (1 c) sour cream
120 ml (1/2 c) fresh lime juice
120 ml (1/2 c) melon liqueur
15 ml (1 tbsp) chopped, fresh spearmint

Put all ingredients into a large mixing bowl and whisk well.

Refrigerate for at least 4 hours.

Whisk again before serving.

Enoki Mushroom and Pea
Serves 6 – 8

240 ml (1 c) dried, black-eyed peas
2 1/2 L (10 c) chicken stock
240 ml (1 c) enoki mushrooms, remove the mushrooms from the main stock with stems intact
240 ml (1 c) thinly sliced onion
240 ml (1 c) thinly sliced green pepper
2 large garlic cloves, sliced
15 ml (1 tbsp) Hoisin sauce
2 eggs, beaten

Soak peas in a large bowl of cold water for 4 hours.

Heat stock at high heat in your soup pot.

Add peas to the stock – after draining off water – and bring to the boil.

Reduce heat and simmer for 2 hours.

Add mushrooms and all other ingredients except eggs and return to the boil for 10 minutes.

Whisk beaten eggs into the broth before serving.

Tomato with Couscous
Serves 6 – 8

60 ml (1/4 c) extra virgin olive oil
120 ml (1/2 c) diced onion
120 ml (1/2 c) diced green pepper
120 ml (1/2 c) diced leek
15 ml (1 tbsp) fresh chopped garlic
320 ml (1 1/2 c) couscous
1 1/2 L (6 c) tomato concassée
240 ml (1 c) chicken or vegetable stock
30 ml (2 tbsp) tomato paste
60 ml (1/4 c) chopped fresh basil

Add olive oil to a heavy soup pot on high heat, stir-frying onions, green pepper and leek for 5 to 6 minutes.

Add garlic and cook another 2 minutes.

Add couscous, concassée, stock, tomato paste and basil.

Bring to the boil, cover, reduce heat, and simmer 10 minutes.

Greek Eggplant
Serves 8

45 ml (3 tbsp) olive oil
1 L (4 c) coarsely diced eggplant
120 ml (1/2 c) sliced leeks
3 garlic cloves, minced
240 ml (1 c) sliced stuffed pimento olives
15 ml (1 tbsp) chopped fresh oregano
2 L (8 c) chicken stock
230 g (1/2 lb) feta cheese, crumbled
Juice of **1** lemon (or to taste)

Heat olive oil in a medium soup pot over medium heat.

Add eggplant, leek, garlic, olives and oregano and sweat for 8 to 10 minutes, stirring frequently.

Add stock and bring to the boil.

Reduce heat and simmer 3 to 4 minutes.

Whisk in cheese and season with lemon juice.

Ground Pork Szechuan
Serves 4 – 6

60 ml (1/4 c) peanut or soybean oil
460 g (1 lb) ground pork
120 ml (1/2 c) julienned red peppers
120 ml (1/2 c) coarsely chopped celery, cut on the diagonal
3 garlic cloves, minced
120 ml (1/2 c) sliced onion
60 ml (1/4 c) sliced leek
5 ml (1 tsp) Hoisin sauce
Pinch of five-spice powder
15 ml (1 tbsp) ketchup
15 ml (1 tbsp) soy sauce
45 ml (3 tbsp) Vietnamese chili sauce
720 ml (3 c) chicken stock
30 ml (2 tbsp) "whitewash" (equal parts cornstarch and water)

Heat oil in a large wok or soup pot over high heat.

Add pork and brown while stirring constantly for 6 to 8 minutes.

Add red pepper, celery, garlic, onion and leek and sauté for 2 to 3 minutes while stirring constantly.

Stir in Hoisin, five-spice powder, ketchup, soy sauce and chili sauce and then add stock.

Bring to the boil and stir in "whitewash" mixture.

Reduce heat and simmer 2 minutes or until thickened slightly.

Potato Dijon
Serves 6 – 8

2 L (8 c) chicken stock
720 ml (3 c) peeled, diced russet potato – **1 cm (1/2 in)** cubes
240 ml (1 c) diced leek, white part only
120 ml (1/2 c) finely diced turnip
60 ml (1/4 c) finely chopped carrot
60 ml (1/4 c) Dijon mustard
60 ml (1/4 c) 35% cream

Combine all ingredients except cream in your soup pot on high heat.

Bring to the boil, and cook at a slow boil for 30 minutes, or until all vegetables are tender.

Whisk in cream.

Return briefly to the boil before serving.

Chow Mein Soup with Pork
Serves 8 – 10

2 L (8 c) chicken stock
230 g (1/2 lb) sliced barbecued pork
1 L (4 c) bean sprouts
240 ml (1 c) sliced onion
240 ml (1 c) sliced green peppers
15 ml (1 tbsp) diced garlic

30 ml (1 oz) soy sauce
15 ml (1 tbsp) diced fresh ginger

In a medium-sized soup pot, bring chicken stock to a rolling boil.

Add all other ingredients, return to the boil, and cook 3 to 4 minutes.

Morels in Broth
Serves 6 – 8

60 ml (1/4 c) clarified butter
460 g (1 lb) fresh morel mushrooms, sliced
120 ml (1/2 c) diced shallots
120 ml (1/2 c) diced leek
15 ml (1 tbsp) chopped garlic
230 g (1/2 lb) double-smoked pork (whole)
2 L (8 c) beef stock

Heat butter in your soup pot on high heat.

Add mushrooms, shallots, leek and garlic and sauté approximately 5 minutes while stirring.

Add pork and stock, bringing the soup to a slow boil.

Reduce heat and simmer for 30 minutes more.

Remove pork before serving.

Lentils with Smoked Pork and Strawberries
Serves 6 – 8

60 ml (1/4 c) clarified butter
240 ml (1 c) diced double-smoked bacon
240 ml (1 c) sliced chanterelle mushrooms
120 ml (1/2 c) sliced leek
120 ml (1/2 c) diced green pepper
120 ml (1/2 c) diced fennel
1 garlic clove, minced
120 ml (1/2 c) sliced celery
120 ml (1/2 c) diced onion
60 ml (1/4 c) brandy
15 ml (1 tbsp) chopped fresh rosemary
480 ml (2 c) sliced strawberries
120 ml (1/2 c) dried lentils
2 L (8 c) chicken stock

Heat butter in a large soup pot.

Add bacon, chanterelles, leek, green pepper, fennel, garlic, celery and onion and sauté for 5 minutes.

Add brandy, then stir in rosemary, strawberries, lentils and stock.

Bring to the boil, then reduce the heat to simmer and cook 45 minutes.

Scallops with Two Mushrooms in Red Wine
Serves 4

1 5-g packet (1/6-oz) dried yellow
   bolete mushrooms
1 5-g packet (1/6-oz) dried cep
   mushrooms
80 ml (1/3 c) red wine
30 ml (2 tbsp) cognac
60 ml (1/4 c) clarified butter
460 g (1 lb) bay scallops
120 ml (1/2 c) diced onion
120 ml (1/2 c) diced pimento or
   red pepper
1 garlic clove, minced
5 ml (1 tsp) chopped fresh tarragon
720 ml (3 c) chicken stock
30 ml (2 tbsp) beurre manié
60 ml (1/4 c) 35% cream

Soak mushrooms in wine and cognac for 1 hour.

Heat the butter in a medium-sized soup pot over medium-high heat.

Add scallops, onion, pimento and garlic and sauté for 3 to 4 minutes.

Add mushrooms, wine and cognac and simmer until reduced by half.

Stir in tarragon and stock and bring to the boil.

Meanwhile, in a small bowl, whisk beurre manié until smooth.

Slowly whisk one cupful of soup into the beurre manié and then whisk the mixture into the soup.

Stir in cream.

Cream of Brussels Sprouts and Gorgonzola
Serves 4 – 6

80 ml (1/3 c) clarified butter
230 g (1/2 lb) Brussels sprouts,
   trimmed
240 ml (1 c) chopped onion
1 L (4 c) chicken stock
60 ml (1/4 c) vermicelli
80 ml (1/3 c) 35% cream
60 ml (1/4 c) crumbled Gorgonzola
Pepper to taste

Heat **45 ml (3 tbsp)** of the butter in a small saucepan.

Add Brussels sprouts and cook for 10 to 15 minutes over medium heat.

Heat remaining butter in a medium-sized soup pot, add onion and sauté for 4 to 5 minutes.

Add the stock to the onion and simmer for 10 minutes.

Add Brussels sprouts and the vermicelli and simmer until noodles are fully cooked.

Stir in cream and Gorgonzola.

Braised Garlic Bordelaise

Serves 4 – 6

1 beef shank (ask your butcher to cut the shank into **2 1/2 cm (1 in)** thick pieces)
30 ml (2 tbsp) clarified butter
120 ml (1/2 c) chopped onion
120 ml (1/2 c) diced green pepper
120 ml (1/2 c) diced leek
14 garlic cloves, peeled
60 ml (1/4 c) Port wine
15 ml (1 tbsp) green peppercorns in brine
1 3/4 L (7 c) beef stock
30 ml (2 tbsp) chopped fresh thyme

Place the beef bones in a medium-sized roasting pan and roast in a preheated 200° C (400° F) oven for 20 to 30 minutes, then remove and cool.

In a medium soup pot, heat butter and sauté onion, green pepper and leek for 4 to 5 minutes, stirring frequently.

Add garlic, Port, green peppercorns, stock and thyme.

Bring to the boil, then reduce heat and simmer for 5 minutes.

Separate the marrow from the beef bones and add marrow to the broth.

Serve 2 to 3 cloves of garlic with each serving.

Fresh Tuna with Whole Capers and Sherry

Serves 4

60 ml (1/4 c) clarified butter
460 g (1 lb) fresh tuna, cut into **1 cm (1/2 in)** chunks
120 ml (1/2 c) chopped onion
1 garlic clove, minced
5 ml (1 tsp) chopped fresh tarragon
35 capers
60 ml (1/4 c) dry sherry
1 L (4 c) chicken stock
45 ml (3 tbsp) beurre manié
60 ml (1/4 c) 35% cream
5 ml (1 tsp) Dijon mustard
Salt, pepper and nutmeg to taste

Melt butter in a medium-sized soup pot over medium heat.

Add tuna and sauté for 2 to 3 minutes.

Add onion, garlic, tarragon and capers and sauté 2 to 3 minutes more.

Stir in sherry and stock and bring to a boil.

Meanwhile, whisk beurre manié until smooth.

Whisk a cupful of soup into beurre manié until a smooth paste is formed then whisk this mixture back into the soup one spoonful at a time.

Stir in the cream and mustard and add salt, pepper and nutmeg to taste.

Shrimp Bisque
Serves 2 – 4

30 ml (2 tbsp) clarified butter
60 ml (1/4 c) diced carrot
60 ml (1/4 c) chopped onion
15 ml (1 tbsp) chopped fresh parsley
5 ml (1 tsp) chopped fresh tarragon
1 bay leaf
460 g (1 lb) prawns, peeled and
   deveined
15 ml (1 tbsp) Armagnac
240 ml (1 c) dry white wine
120 ml (1/2 c) long grain rice
720 ml (3 c) chicken stock
80 ml (1/3 c) 35% cream

Melt butter in a heavy soup pot over medium-high heat.

Add carrot, onion, parsley, tarragon and bay leaf and sauté about 4 minutes or until golden brown.

Add prawns and cook for a couple of minutes.

Sprinkle with Armagnac, stir in wine and **125 ml (1/2 cup)** stock.

Simmer for 3 minutes until slightly reduced.

In a separate pot cook the rice in the remaining stock by bringing it to a boil, then simmering for 15 to 20 minutes.

Stir the cooked rice into the soup, and whisk in cream.

West Indian Pepperpot
Serves 8 – 10

680 g (1 1/2 lbs) short ribs, 1/2 cm
   (1/4 in) thick, cut into **5 cm (2 in)**
   pieces
120 ml (1/2 c) red wine
2 large carrots, peeled and sliced
1 large potato, peeled and diced
2 Scotch bonnet peppers
120 ml (1/2 c) diced green pepper
120 ml (1/2 c) sliced leek
1 garlic clove, minced
3 anise stars
1 small cinnamon stick
5 ml (1 tsp) finely chopped thyme
2 1/2 L (10 c) cold water
30 ml (2 tbsp) long grain white or
   brown rice

Roast short ribs in a preheated 180° C (350° F) oven for 30 minutes or until browned.

Deglaze the roasting pan with red wine.

Place short ribs, wine, carrot, potato, peppers, leek, garlic, anise, cinnamon, thyme and water into a large soup pot and bring to a boil.

Reduce heat and simmer for 40 to 50 minutes.

Add the rice and simmer another 20 minutes.

Old Fashioned Corn Chowder
Serves 6

45 ml (3 tbsp) clarified butter
720 ml (3 c) corn niblets
 (about 6 cobs of corn)
120 ml (1/2 c) sliced celery
120 ml (1/2 c) diced red pepper
120 ml (1/2 c) diced green pepper
120 ml (1/2 c) chopped onion
1 garlic clove, minced
1 L (4 c) chicken stock
60 ml (1/4 c) beurre manié
120 ml (1/2 c) 35% cream
15 ml (1 tbsp) brown sugar
3 dashes Worcestershire sauce
Pinch dry mustard
Pinch nutmeg
Salt and pepper to taste

Heat butter in medium-sized soup pot over medium heat.

Add corn, celery, peppers, onion and garlic and sauté for 4 to 5 minutes.

Add chicken stock and bring to the boil.

Reduce heat and simmer 8 to 10 minutes.

Meanwhile, in a small bowl whisk the beurre manié until it is smooth. Slowly whisk in a cupful of soup until a smooth mixture is formed and slowly whisk this mixture back into the soup one spoonful at a time while whisking steadily.

Stir in cream and brown sugar and season with Worcestershire, mustard, nutmeg and salt and pepper to taste.

Spanish Onion and Bean
Serves 6 – 8

240 ml (1 c) dried white beans
2 garlic cloves, minced
60 ml (1/4 c) lard
120 ml (1/2 c) chopped Spanish
 onion
1 small cabbage shredded
2 3/4 L (11 c) beef stock

In a large, non-metallic bowl, cover beans and garlic with cold water and soak overnight.

Heat lard in a medium-sized soup pot over medium-high heat.

Add the onion and sauté for 3 to 4 minutes, stirring occasionally.

Add cabbage, drained beans with the garlic and the stock.

Bring to a boil, then reduce heat and simmer about 3 hours or until beans are tender.

Bouillabaise
Serves 4

30 ml (2 tbsp) clarified butter
120 ml (1/2 c) whole leeks, diced
120 ml (1/2 c) diced shallots
2 cloves of garlic, minced
10 whole capers
240 ml (1 c) mushrooms, sliced
3 large tomatoes, peeled, seeded
   and chopped
15 ml (1 tbsp) sugar
15 threads saffron
240 ml (1 c) dry white wine
60 ml (1/4 c) cognac
230 g (1/2 lb) mussels in their shells
12 little neck clams in their shells
10 ml (2 tsp) chopped fresh tarragon
10 green peppercorns (dried)
10 fennel seeds
230 g (1/2 lb) red snapper cut into
   6 pieces (including bones and skin)
230 g (1/2 lb) King crab legs cut into
   8 pieces
1 medium lobster tail (cut into
   4 pieces)
480 ml (2 c) clear fish stock

Heat butter in a large sauté pan over medium-high heat.

Add leek, shallots, garlic, capers and mushrooms and cook approximately 4 minutes, or until vegetables are limp.

Add tomatoes, sugar and saffron and continue cooking 10 minutes more.

Add white wine and cognac.

Bring to a boil and add mussels and clams, cooking about 3 minutes, or until shells have opened.

Add tarragon, green peppercorns, fennel seeds, snapper, crab and lobster.

Cook with lid on for about 3 minutes or until seafood is cooked through.

Add fish stock and bring to a boil before serving.

Lamb Porcini
Serves 6 – 8

30 g (1 oz) dried porcini mushrooms
80 ml (1/3 c) red wine
60 ml (1/4 c) clarified butter
680 g (1 1/2 lbs) lamb, cut into
   1 cm (1/2 in) cubes
1 garlic clove minced
120 ml (1/2 c) diced onion
120 ml (1/2 c) diced leek
120 ml (1/2 c) diced green pepper
5 ml (1 tsp) fresh chopped thyme
3 bay leaves
1 1/2 L (6 c) lamb or beef stock
60 ml (1/4 c) pearly barley
240 ml (1 c) tomato sauce
120 ml (1/2 c) chopped sun-dried
   tomatoes

Cover mushrooms with wine and let soak 1 hour.

Heat butter in medium-sized soup pot.

Add the lamb and brown, stirring occasionally.

Add garlic, onion, leek, green pepper, thyme, and bay leaves and sauté 2 to 3 minutes while stirring occasionally.

Add mushrooms, wine and stock and bring to a boil.

Reduce heat to a simmer and stir in the barley, tomato sauce and sun-dried tomatoes.

Simmer 20 to 30 minutes.

Hungarian Cabbage with Ground Beef
Serves 8 – 10

60 ml (1/4 c) olive oil
460 g (1 lb) lean ground beef
3 garlic cloves, minced
120 ml (1/2 c) diced onion
120 ml (1/2 c) diced green pepper
120 ml (1/2 c) diced red pepper
120 ml (1/2 c) chopped leek
1 1/4 L (5 c) shredded cabbage
120 ml (1/2 c) white wine sauerkraut, drained
120 ml (1/2 c) long grain white rice
480 ml (2 c) tomato sauce
2 L (8 c) chicken stock

Heat oil in a medium-sized soup pot.

Add ground beef and cook 5 to 6 minutes while stirring until browned.

Add garlic, onion, peppers, leek, cabbage, sauerkraut and rice and continue to sauté for 3 to 4 minutes.

Add tomato sauce and stock and bring to a boil.

Reduce heat and simmer for 20 minutes.

Coq-a-Leekie
Serves 6

60 ml (1/4 c) clarified butter
460 g (1 lb) diced raw chicken
1 L (4 c) diced leeks
120 ml (1/2 c) diced red pepper
15 ml (1 tbsp) raw long grain rice
30 ml (2 tbsp) diced garlic
1 1/2 L (6 c) chicken stock
120 ml (1/2 c) 35% cream

Heat butter in a heavy soup pot on high heat.

Add chicken, leek and peppers and cook on high heat for approximately 5 minutes while stirring.

Add rice, garlic and chicken stock and bring to a boil.

Reduce heat, stir in cream, and simmer, covered, for 20 minutes.

Belgian Endive with Lemon, Lime and Cream
Serves 4 – 6

45 ml (3 tbsp) clarified butter
120 ml (1/2 c) chopped onion
60 ml (1/4 c) diced red pepper
15 ml (1 tbsp) chopped fresh dill
1 L (4 c) chicken stock
Juice of **1** lemon
Juice of **2** limes
720 ml (3 c) sliced Belgian endive
60 ml (1/4 c) beurre manié
80 ml (1/3 c) 35% cream

Heat butter over medium heat in your soup pot.

Add onion, pepper and dill and sauté 3 to 4 minutes.

Add stock, lemon and lime juices and Belgian endive.

Bring to the boil and cook for 2 to 3 minutes.

Meanwhile, in a small bowl, whisk the beurre manié to a smooth texture. Slowly whisk in a cupful of soup then whisk that mixture back into the soup 1 spoonful at a time.

Simmer soup 3 to 4 minutes or until thickened slightly.

Stir in cream.

Nutmeg, salt and pepper may be added to taste.

Crab a la King
Serves 8

60 ml (1/4 c) clarified butter
1 garlic clove, minced
120 ml (1/2 c) diced onion
30 stuffed green olives
120 ml (1/2 c) diced green pepper
900 g (2 lbs) king crab legs cut into **5 cm (2 in)** pieces
120 ml (1/2 c) chopped fresh basil
60 ml (1/4 c) dry white wine
60 ml (1/4 c) dry red wine
1 1/2 L (6 c) chicken stock
60 ml (1/4 c) beurre manié
80 ml (1/3 c) 35% cream
120 ml (1/2 c) grated Romano cheese

Heat butter in a large soup pot.

Add garlic, onion, olives and green pepper and sauté for 2 minutes.

Add the crab and basil and sauté for 2 to 3 minutes more while stirring occasionally.

Add wine and stock and bring to the boil.

Meanwhile, whisk beurre manié in a medium-sized bowl until smooth, then whisk a cupful of soup into the beurre manié.

Add this mixture back into the soup 1 spoonful at a time.

Whisk in cream and cheese and simmer 2 to 3 minutes before serving.

Spicy Spanish Chorizo

Serves 4 – 6

60 ml (1/4 c) clarified butter
120 ml (1/2 c) sliced onion
120 ml (1/2 c) julienned green pepper
1 garlic clove, minced
120 ml (1/2 c) sliced celery
6 dried chili peppers
480 ml (2 c) sliced dried chorizo sausage
6 fennel seeds
10 ml (2 tsp) chopped fresh coriander
720 ml (3 c) fresh tomato sauce
480 ml (2 c) chicken stock

Heat butter in a medium-sized soup pot.

Add onions, pepper, garlic celery and chili peppers and sauté for 4 to 5 minutes, stirring occasionally.

Add sausage, fennel seeds, coriander, tomato sauce and chicken stock and bring to the boil.

Reduce heat and simmer 8 to 10 minutes.

English Stew with Ground Beef

Serves 3 – 4

120 ml (1/2 c) clarified butter
680 g (1 1/2 lbs) lean ground beef
120 ml (1/2 c) tomato concassée
120 ml (1/2 c) diced green pepper
120 ml (1/2 c) diced carrot
120 ml (1/2 c) diced onion
120 ml (1/2 c) diced leek
1 garlic clove, minced
2 ml (1/2 tsp) chopped thyme
1 L (4 c) beef stock
15 ml (1 tbsp) Dijon mustard
120 ml (1/2 c) sour cream

Melt butter in a medium soup pot on medium temperature.

Add beef and cook 8 to 10 minutes, stirring occasionally until all meat is browned.

Add tomato concassée, green pepper, carrot, onion, leek and garlic and sauté for 4 to 5 minutes.

Add thyme and beef stock, bring to the boil, then reduce heat and simmer 8 to 10 minutes.

Whisk in mustard.

Serve in soup bowls and top each bowl with a dollop of sour cream.

Clear Tomato
Serves 4

1 1/4 L (5 c) beef broth
4 large, ripe tomatoes, chopped
345 g (3/4 lb) lean ground beef
240 ml (1 c) chopped leeks
120 ml (1/2 c) chopped celery
120 ml (1/2 c) Madeira wine
Salt and pepper to taste.

Place all ingredients – except Madeira – into your soup pot and simmer for 1 hour.

Strain through cheesecloth or very fine sieve.

Add Madeira, stir, and serve.

Cold Zucchini with Curry
Serves 6

900 g (2 lbs) coarsely chopped zucchini
1 large onion, coarsely chopped
2 cloves of garlic, chopped
5 ml (1 tsp) curry powder
720 ml (3 c) chicken stock
240 ml (1 c) sour cream
120 ml (1/2 c) fresh chives, chopped for garnish

Place all ingredients except the sour cream and chives into a large soup pot and cook on medium heat for 10 to 12 minutes, or until vegetables are tender.

Allow the soup to cool, then purée in a blender.

Chill four hours.

Stir in sour cream before serving.

Top each helping with a sprinkle of chives.

Chilled Pineapple and Strawberry with Kirsch
Serves 8 – 10

1 L (4 c) strawberries, hulled and washed
240 ml (1 c) pineapple, peeled and cut into chunks
240 ml (1 c) sour cream
720 ml (3 c) 10% cream
10 ml (2 tsp) white sugar
45 ml (3 tbsp) chopped fresh dill
80 ml (1/3 c) Kirsch

Whir the strawberries and pineapple in the bowl of a food processor until smooth – approximately 3 minutes.

Place the sour cream in a large bowl and slowly whisk in the fruit purée.

Whisk in the 10% cream and the seasoning of sugar, dill and Kirsch.

Chill before serving.

Maritime
Fish Chowder
Serves 6

900 g (2 lbs) fresh haddock
30 ml (2 tbsp) Pernod
60 g (2 oz) diced salt pork
2 medium onions, coarsely chopped
4 large potatoes, coarsely chopped
240 ml (1 c) chopped celery
1 bay leaf
1 1/4 L (5 c) whole milk

Simmer haddock in **480 ml (2 c)** of water plus the Pernod for 15 minutes and set aside to debone when it cools. (Save the liquid from this step.)

While fish is cooling, sauté the diced pork in a large skillet until crisp and set aside.

Add the onions to the pork fat and sauté until golden brown.

Add the fish broth, the fish (minus its bones), the onion, potatoes, celery and bay leaf into the skillet and cook in the fish broth until the potatoes are tender.

Add the milk and return briefly to the boil before serving.

Top each serving with a sprinkle of pork crisps.

Chilled
Beet Greens
Serves 6

420 ml (1 3/4 c) chopped beet greens
120 ml (1/2 c) water
30 ml (2 tbsp) butter
2 medium onions, chopped
2 potatoes, peeled and cooked
1 L (4 c) chicken broth
240 ml (1 c) milk
Salt and pepper to taste
60 ml (1/4 c) cooked, diced beets
6 very thin lemon slices

Cook beet greens in water for 10 to 15 minutes and drain.

Sweat the onions in butter until transparent.

Purée cooked greens, cooked potato, onion and 3 cups of chicken broth in blender.

Put purée into your soup pot, add final cup of broth and simmer 5 minutes.

Stir in milk and seasoning and refrigerate approximately 4 hours until chilled.

Garnish individual servings with diced beets and slices of lemon.

Manhattan Clam Chowder

Serves 6 – 8

12 cherrystone clams
480 ml (2 c) clam juice
1 slice bacon
2 medium onions, diced
2 medium potatoes, diced
10 ml (2 tsp) minced garlic
4 medium tomatoes, peeled, seeded
   and chopped
30 ml (2 tbsp) fresh thyme, chopped
1 L (4 c) chicken stock

Steam the clams in the clam juice in a large soup pot about 5 minutes, or until they open.

Set clams aside to cool and strain broth to remove any sand or grit.

Cook bacon in a large saucepan on low heat so that fat is rendered but bacon remains limp and does not crisp or brown.

Discard bacon, adding onion, potato and garlic to the bacon fat and cook slowly for approximately 10 minutes, or until onions are soft and translucent.

Add tomato and thyme and cook for approximately 1 minute more while stirring.

Add the above to stock in a medium-sized soup pot.

Add clam broth and bring the chowder to a simmer for 5 minutes, or until potato is tender.

Remove clams from shells and dice them and add them to the chowder.

Simmer briefly and serve.

Leek and Mustard

Serves 6

60 ml (1/4 c) clarified butter
1 L (4 c) diced leek, white
   stem only
1 garlic clove, chopped
1 1/2 L (6 c) chicken stock
60 ml (1/4 c) uncooked orzo noodles
240 ml (1 c) chopped fresh spinach
60 ml (1/4 c) Dijon mustard

Melt the butter in a medium-sized soup pot on high heat.

Add leeks and cook 5 minutes while stirring.

Add garlic and cook another 5 minutes while stirring occasionally.

Add chicken stock and bring to the boil.

Add pasta.

Reduce heat to simmer, cover soup pot, and cook 8 to 10 minutes.

Add spinach and continue cooking approximately 2 minutes more.

Stir in mustard.

Split Pea
Serves 8

460 g (1 lb) split peas, green or yellow
1 smoked pork hock
1 large onion, peeled and left whole
2 carrots, peeled and left whole
2 ribs of celery left whole
1 bay leaf
5 ml (1 tsp) thyme
5 ml (1 tsp) sage
Salt and black pepper to taste
240 ml (1 c) milk
Croutons for garnish

Put all ingredients except milk and croutons into a large soup pot.

Add **8 cups** of cold water and bring slowly to a boil.

Reduce heat and simmer 3 to 4 hours, or until peas have completely disintegrated.

Using a slotted spoon, remove the onion, carrots, celery and bay leaf and discard.

Remove the pork hock and after removing the fatty skin, shred the meat finely, away from the bone and return it to the soup mixture.

Add milk while stirring briskly and return to a low boil.

Top individual servings with croutons.

Italian Onion
Serves 8 – 10

60 ml (1/4 c) extra virgin olive oil
1 L (4 c) sliced red onion
240 ml (1 c) diced leek greens
60 ml (1/4 c) thinly sliced fresh garlic
30 ml (2 tbsp) fresh chopped oregano
480 ml (2 c) beef stock
2 L (8 c) tomato purée
240 ml (1 c) grated Tuscanello cheese

Heat oil in a heavy soup pot on high.

When oil begins to smoke add onion and leek and cook on high heat until onion begins to brown.

Add garlic and continue cooking until garlic turns a golden brown.

Add oregano and stock and bring slowly to a boil.

Add tomato purée and return to the boil.

Reduce heat and simmer, covered, for 30 minutes stirring occasionally.

Garnish each serving with grated cheese.

Champagne Lemon
Serves 4 – 6

720 ml (3 c) 35% cream
4 strands saffron
30 ml (2 tbsp) white sugar
480 ml (2 c) chicken velouté
240 ml (1 c) lemon juice
Zest from **3** lemons
480 ml (2 c) champagne

Bring cream to a boil in your soup pot and add saffron.

Reduce to a simmer and reduce mixture by half.

Add sugar and velouté and return to the boil.

Add lemon juice and zest.

Return to a boil briefly and add champagne before serving.

Corn St. Agur
Serves 6 – 8

2 L (8 c) chicken stock
480–720 ml (2–3 c) kernels from **6** cobs of corn
120 ml (1/2 c) diced onion
15 ml (1 tbsp) diced garlic
60 ml (1/4 c) roasted red peppers, diced
30 ml (2 tbsp) green peppercorns in brine

115 g (1/4 lb) shredded St. Agur cheese

Place stock, corn, onions and garlic in a medium-sized soup pot and bring to a boil.

Reduce heat and simmer 30 minutes.

Add peppers and peppercorns and return to the boil.

Whisk in St. Agur until completely melted.

Kippers and Brie
Serves 4 – 6

115 g (1/4 lb) boned, chopped kippers
115 g (1/4 lb) peeled Brie
720 ml (3 c) 35% cream
2 ml (1/2 tsp) chopped tarragon
30 ml (2 tbsp) kosher salt
Chopped chervil for garnish
Whipped cream

Bring all ingredients (except chervil and whipped cream) to a boil in your soup pot.

Reduce heat to medium and reduce mixture by a third.

Remove from heat and let stand approximately 2 minutes before serving.

Garnish with chopped chervil and a dollop of whipped cream.

Flank Steak with Hoisin and Pepper
Serves 4

60 ml (1/4 c) peanut oil
680 g (1 1/2 lbs) flank steak
  cut into thin strips
120 ml (1/2 c) julienned leek
120 ml (1/2 c) julienned green
  pepper
120 ml (1/2 c) julienned red pepper
30 ml (2 tbsp) julienned jalapeno
  pepper
1 garlic clove, minced
5 ml (1 tsp) finely chopped fresh
  ginger
Juice of **1/2** lemon
Pinch of five-spice powder
15 ml (1 tbsp) Hoisin sauce
15 ml (1 tbsp) Vietnamese chili sauce
720 ml (3 c) beef stock
30 ml (2 tbsp) beurre manié

Heat oil in medium-sized pot
over medium high heat.

Stir-fry steak for 2 to 3 minutes
while stirring constantly.

Add leek, peppers, garlic and
ginger, stir-frying 2 to 3 minutes
more.

Add lemon juice, pinch of
five-spice powder, Hoisin, chili
sauce and stock.

Mix beurre manié into cup of
soup broth until smooth then
stir mixture into soup 1 spoonful
at a time.

Cook on medium high heat
2 to 3 minutes, or until slightly
thickened.

Apple and Yam
Serves 6 – 8

1 L (4 c) peeled, cored, sliced
  spy apples
1 L (4 c) peeled, chopped yams
120 ml (1/2 c) demerara sugar
1/2 cinnamon stick
120 ml (1/2 c) 35% cream
120 ml (4 oz) bourbon
30 ml (2 tbsp) kosher salt

Bring apples, yams and sugar
to a boil in a pot of water on
high heat.

Reduce heat, add cinnamon
and simmer 35 to 40 minutes.

Strain and remove cinnamon.

Purée the yams and apples in
your blender.

Pour puréed yams and apples
into your soup pot.

Stir in cream, bourbon and salt.

Re-heat to serving temperature
while stirring.

Shrimp and Garlic with Mushroom Caps and Pernod

Serves 4 – 6

Stock

680 g (1 1/2 lbs) jumbo shrimp, peeled, cleaned and chopped into **3** pieces each (reserve shells for stock)
1 1/2 L (6 c) chicken stock
3 bay leaves

Soup

60 ml (1/4 c) unsalted butter
20 medium-sized mushroom caps
240 ml (1 c) finely diced onion
15 ml (1 tbsp) minced garlic
30 ml (2 tbsp) diced pimento or sweet red bell pepper
5 ml (1 tsp) dried tarragon
5 ml (1 tsp) curry powder
120 ml (1/2 c) dry white wine
30 ml (2 tbsp) Pernod

Approximately **1 1/4 L (5 c)** of quick-and-easy shrimp stock can be made by bringing the shrimp shells together with the chicken stock, onion and bay leaves to a rolling boil, then reducing heat and simmering for 30 minutes. (The stock can become bitter if simmered longer.)

Strain and set the stock aside.

In a medium-sized soup pot, melt the butter and sauté the mushrooms about 4 minutes.

Add the shrimp, onion, garlic, pimento, tarragon and curry powder and sauté an additional 5 to 7 minutes until onions are soft.

Stir in white wine, bring to a boil and reduce by approximately half by allowing to boil uncovered about 10 minutes.

Stir in shrimp stock and Pernod and return to the boiling point before serving.

Red Cabbage and Pork

Serves 8

60 ml (1/4 c) butter
480 ml (2 c) shredded red cabbage
120 ml (1/2 c) diced onion
60 ml (1/4 c) diced green pepper
60 ml (1/4 c) diced leek (white stem only)
15 ml (1 tbsp) diced garlic
115 g (1/4 lb) double-smoked bacon cut into **1/2 cm (1/4 in)** pieces
6 juniper berries
15 ml (1 tbsp) chopped fresh rosemary
1 1/2 L (6 c) chicken stock

Put all ingredients, including stock, into your soup pot and bring to a rolling boil.

Reduce heat and simmer, covered, for 10 to 12 minutes.

Chilled Elderberry with Smoked Salmon
Serves 6 – 8

120 ml (1/2 c) elderberry jam
480 ml (2 c) sour cream
240 ml (1 c) 35% cream
30 ml (2 tbsp) lemon zest
120 ml (1/2 c) Cassis liqueur
15 ml (1 tbsp) fresh chopped mint
230 g (1/2 lb) julienne of smoked salmon
240 ml (1 c) cocktail shrimps

Put all ingredients except salmon and shrimp into a large mixing bowl and whisk well.

Gently stir salmon and shrimp into the mix.

Cover and refrigerate 4 – 5 hours.

Cheese with Leek
Serves 4

780 ml (3 1/4 c) 35% cream
60 ml (1/4 c) grated cheddar
60 ml (1/4 c) grated Tuscanello
60 ml (1/4 c) crumbled Danish blue
60 ml (1/4 c) grated Munster
30 ml (2 tbsp) grated Romano
30 ml (1 oz) brandy
60 ml (1/4 c) lightly sautéed julienne of leek greens

Heat cream to boiling point in medium-sized soup pot.

Reduce cream by one-third at a simmer.

Whisk in all cheeses and stir on medium heat until cheeses are completed melted and blended into the cream.

Add brandy.

Garnish each serving with leeks.

Potato Spinach au Gratin
Serves 6 – 8

480 ml (2 c) potatoes, diced into
 1/2 cm (1/4 in) cubes
60 ml (1/4 c) diced onion
720 ml (3 c) 35% cream
460 g (1 lb) washed, chopped
 spinach
240 ml (1 c) shredded medium
 cheddar
60 ml (1/4 c) grated Parmesan
1 pinch of grated nutmeg

Put potato, onions and cream into your soup pot on high heat and bring to the boil while stirring to avoid potato sticking to pot.

Reduce heat to medium and reduce by 1/4 by simmering 6 to 8 minutes, while continuing to stir.

Return to the boil while adding all other ingredients and stir until cheese is completely melted.

Leek with Tomato and Sour Cream
Serves 6 – 8

60 ml (1/4 c) extra virgin olive oil
1 L (4 c) diced leek, cut into
 1 cm (1/2 in) pieces
15 ml (1 tbsp) chopped fresh garlic
120 ml (1/2 c) diced green pepper
5 ml (1 tsp) fresh oregano
45 ml (3 tbsp) tomato paste
1 L (4 c) tomato concassée
120 ml (1/2 c) sour cream
480 ml (2 c) 35% cream

Heat oil in a heavy soup pot on high heat.

Add leek and stir while cooking 4 to 5 minutes.

Add garlic, green pepper, oregano and tomato paste and continue cooking another 2 to 3 minutes.

With heat still on high, add tomato concassée and bring to the boil while stirring.

Add sour cream and cream, reduce heat and simmer 5 minutes.

Merry, Merry Christmas Mincemeat
Serves 6

720 ml (3 c) mincemeat pie filling
60 ml (1/4 c) whole sweet butter
240 ml (1 c) dark rum
240 ml (1 c) brandy
120 ml (1/2 c) Madeira
15 ml (1 tbsp) finely grated
    cinnamon

Place mincemeat into your soup pot on medium-high heat, stirring for 8 to 10 minutes.

Whisk in butter.

Add rum, brandy and Madeira and continue cooking for 2 minutes.

Top each serving with a sprinkle of grated cinnamon.

Casaba Provolone
Serves 6 – 8

120 ml (1/2 c) whole butter
60 ml (1/4 c) diced onion
60 ml (1/4 c) diced green of leek
15 ml (1 tbsp) diced garlic
480 ml (2 c) finely diced casaba
    melon
480 ml (2 c) 35% cream
240 ml (1 c) pork or chicken stock
240 ml (1 c) sauerkraut
60 ml (1 tbsp) caraway seeds
240 ml (1 c) shredded Provolone
    cheese

Melt butter in your soup pot over high heat.

Add onion and leek and stir until the onion begins to brown.

Add garlic while stirring.

Add casaba, cream, stock, sauerkraut and caraway seeds and bring to the boil while stirring 4 to 5 minutes.

Whisk in cheese until completed melted.

Index

NOTES

Page	Recipe	Variations	Comments

NOTES

Page	Recipe	Variations	Comments